Religion and Society

Religion and Society

By ELIZABETH K. NOTTINGHAM

Queens College

BL60
,N91

RANDOM HOUSE
New York

Twelfth Printing, June 1964

To
Christiana

COVER ILLUSTRATION:
A reproduction of a photograph of Henry Moore's "The Family Group."
—Collection The Museum of Modern Art, New York.
—A. Conger Goodyear Fund

LIBRARY OF CONGRESS CATALOG CARD NUMBER 54-11418
MANUFACTURED IN THE UNITED STATES OF AMERICA

Editor's Foreword

What can sociology teach us about religion? Answers to this question—one posed with increasing frequency—may be sought in general textbooks in use today, but the findings are unlikely to be rewarding. Sociological texts more often than not give short shrift to the subject. With one or two notable exceptions, the chapter (convention calls for a chapter, though sometimes it is omitted) on religious institutions or religious organization typically includes a few paragraphs on religion and magic in nonliterate societies, sketchy information on world religions, perhaps brief reference to findings and formulations of the pioneers Durkheim and Weber and Troeltsch, acknowledgment of the interest of religious groups in social problems, and discussion of church membership and organization in the United States. These are all important matters, to be sure, but they are rarely brought together and presented in a manner to suggest answers to our question about *sociology's* contribution to the understanding of religion. This question is paramount in this Short Study.

Religion and Society is unprecedented as an introduction to the sociology of religion. Professor Nottingham draws upon a variety of sources: researches in anthropology, sociology, and history; systematic social theory, especially functional theory, which is used judiciously and which undergirds a clearcut interpretation of religion's social role; landmark studies in the sociology of religion; the author's own observations of religious activities in different cultures; descriptive and even fictional materials, which not only increase the vividness and readability of the analysis but also provide fresh insights uncommon in textbooks.

Professor Nottingham's study illustrates the utility of functional analysis. Functionalism, particularly as it has been developed in the theoretical writings of Talcott Parsons, enriches her discussion of the manifest and less apparent consequences of religion for social integration, for problems of human adjustment, and for social disequilibrium and change. These subjects and that of religious organization are viewed in terms of concrete historical and cultural contexts, a treatment enhanced by the author's extensive use of the three societal types elaborated in Chapter Three.

Undertaking to write a theoretically informed, systematic, yet introductory study of religion and society is a large assignment. Professor Nottingham's successful accomplishment of this task is not surprising in view of her outstanding qualifications. She has been a persistent student of religion for many years, as her publications and teaching in this area indicate. Unlike most contemporary sociologists, her professional training includes intensive study of history as well as sociology, an especially valuable combination for her principal field of interest. These large assets are supplemented by what Cooley termed "sympathetic perception" of human situations and by sensitivity to the needs of student and general readers. Here then is a book marked by scholarly and literary virtues, a work that meets a frequently voiced need of teachers and students.

Works of this order until recently were discouraged in this country by the propensity of various sociologists (themselves often men of theological training) to join in an attack against this or that religious belief or practice and sometimes to decry religion as such in favor of secular science; or in some instances—for example, in the case of Charles A. Ellwood—to seek justification in sociology for support of a particular religious-ethical point of view. However, as Professor Nottingham notes, these efforts have largely disappeared. She joins a growing number of scholars in stressing that the truths of science possess no necessary priority for human beings. At the same time, and in keeping with the values of her profession, she demonstrates that the established and potential findings of social science concerning religion contain significant lessons for believer and nonbeliever alike. Professor Nottingham teaches these lessons well.

CHARLES H. PAGE

Preface

This book seeks to provide the student of sociology and the interested layman with a basic point of view concerning the part played by religion in human societies. Religion is treated in a broad and universal sense, from a social rather than from an individual or theological standpoint. Our inquiry is focused on its functions in furthering or hampering the survival and maintenance of social groups.

A book of this size inevitably raises more questions than it answers, and such answers as it suggests perforce ignore or gloss over many scholarly controversial issues. But we do not try to protect the student from controversial issues. Our aim is to help him face them humbly and honestly. If we furnish intellectual tools with which the student can answer some of his own questions and if we stimulate his interest to carry further his own lines of inquiry into this difficult but fascinating field, we must be content.

The day has all but gone by when social scientists and other intellectuals claim that religion is obsolete and its replacement in human society by a triumphant science is merely a matter of time. The findings of a more mature social science bear impressive testimony to the fact that the social (and psychological) functions performed by religion are fundamental. Indeed, innovating revolutionaries, whether French or Russian, who have tried to banish religion, have succeeded only in renaming it. Conversely, science too may itself be transformed by its latter-day devotees from an empirical discipline to a sacred cow.

Though the march of science has not replaced the basic functions of religion, it has outmoded particular religious manifestations. This fact is of great significance for the student of religion and society. Societies differ from one another markedly in the degree of their scientific and technological development. These differences set a large task for social science: the analysis of different ways in which religion actually performs its functions in diverse types of societies. The task is less ambitious but (in view of available knowledge and techniques) more manageable than the quest for origins pursued by such nineteenth-century thinkers as Herbert Spencer.

The sociologist of religion may or may not be a religious believer. He must, however, be dedicated to the ethics of his science, for him a moral imperative. In this sense Émile Durkheim, Max Weber, and Ernst Troeltsch, three pioneer scholars in the field of religion and society, were dedicated men. Our indebtedness to their studies is conspicuous.

If the laws of gravitation, as established by the natural sciences, are "true," they are true for religious believers and nonbelievers alike. Similarly with the principles of social life—if they can be empirically validated by social science, they should be acceptable to men of all religious faiths or of none. But the sociologist of religion who is himself a religionist faces no logical compulsion to regard his religion as being in conflict with his science. Newton, a sincere Christian, regarded the activities of the natural scientist as religious, and natural laws for him were laws of God. Einstein, too, looks on the discovery of new vistas in an ever-expanding universe as a stimulus to the religious spirit. In the same way it is open to the social scientist to consider emergent social laws, as well as the developing techniques by which he strives to reveal them, as God-given. This is the position of the author of this study. Many, though by no means all, social scientists subscribe to it.

I welcome this opportunity to thank Talcott Parsons whose thought has deeply influenced this analysis of religion and society. And to Charles H. Page, editor of this series, I owe an especial debt for his unstinting help and friendly generous counsel.

ELIZABETH K. NOTTINGHAM

Queens College
Flushing, New York.

Contents

||||||||||||||||||||||||||||||||||||||||||||||||||||||||||||||||||||||||||||||||||||||||||||||||||||||||||||||||||||||||||||||||||||||||||||||||||||

chapter one

A Sociological View of Religion

The Sociologist's Concern with Religion

Since this study is one about religion and sociology, it is appropriate to begin it with a "religious" comparison. A good sociologist and a good Quaker have at least this in common: when they bring their minds to bear on the confused welter of human behavior they try to single out certain things, and certain things only, about which they "have a concern." The cultivation of the capacity of distinguishing what are respectively their essential "concerns" is no mean task whether for Quaker or sociologist.

Because of the richness and variety of its subject matter the field of religion is a difficult one for the exercise of sociological discrimination. For many of us our main interest in religion is personal and individualistic, and in thinking about it we are apt to focus on the more intellectual and emotional aspects of ethics and belief. Like William James we are concerned with the "feelings, acts and experiences of individual men in their solitude . . . in relation to whatsoever they consider the divine."[1] But James, in his definition of religion, left out precisely those universal, societal, and institutional aspects of it that are of the most direct concern of the sociologist. The sociologist's interest is neither that of the philosopher, theologian, nor individual psychologist. He is interested in religion as a universal function of human societies wherever they may be found. His concern is with religion as an aspect of group behavior and with the roles religion has played through the ages, and still plays, in furthering —and hampering—the survival of human groups. The less individual and the more universal, the less unusual and the more repetitive, the behavior under observation, the more likely it is to be grist to the sociologist's mill.

The universality of religious behavior among human beings may for practical purposes be assumed. The earliest relics of Neanderthal man show evidences of activities that have been interpreted by scholars as religious. No modern ethnologist has yet discovered a human group without traces of behavior that may be similarly described. Difficult as this universality may be to explain (a problem to which we shall return later), it is an established historical and anthropological fact. Hence the sociologist is faced with the problem of finding a definition of religion suitable for his particular purposes, namely one which is sufficiently specific to furnish a useful tool for the understanding of social life and yet broad enough to be applicable to the religious behavior of "all sorts and conditions of men."

Religion and the Condition of Man

We are the first to admit that no definition really satisfies. For one thing, religion in its almost unimaginable variety calls for description rather than definition. It is a phenomenon so much "in the round" that it yields reluctantly to our attempts at scientific abstraction. Religion is associated with man's attempts to plumb the depths of meaning in both himself and the universe. It has given rise to the most spacious products of his imagination, and it has been used to justify the extremest cruelty of man to man. It can conjure up moods of the most sublime exaltation, and also images of dread and terror. Though preoccupied with the reality of a world which cannot be seen, religion has been involved with the most mundane details of daily life. It has been used to blaze new trails into the heart of the unknown, and utopias have been founded in its name; yet it has served to bind upon the backs of men outworn shackles of custom or belief.

Worship in common—the sharing of the symbols of religion—has united human groups in the closest ties known to man, yet religious differences have helped to account for some of the fiercest group antagonisms. Religious worship has been adorned with all the exuberance of the arts; it has also flourished under conditions of the barest austerity. Religion has provided men with symbols whereby they may express the inexpressible, yet the essence of the religious experience forever eludes expression. The thought of God has served to encourage men in the tasks of everyday, to reconcile them to an unkind fate, or again, to "take up arms against a sea of troubles and by opposing end them." Paradox is at its heart, for as men have sought to plumb the mystery of things they have perforce attempted to understand and reconcile the great polarities of the universe and in themselves: good and evil, love and loathing, worship and dread, god and devil.

What does all this mean to the student of society? Though he can never be indifferent to the problems presented by the essential nature of religion itself, his special concern is, of course, with religion as manifested in *human be-havior*. In this more limited area he has problems in plenty. A preliminary one is likely to be an understanding of his own attitudes. For people in any society the conception of religion held is so much part and parcel of their particular way of life, so colored by their special feeling for what they consider sacred, that it is hard even for us moderns to look at religion with an impartial scientific eye. In our Western society, religion is closely bound up with our most cherished ideals, with a belief in One God, in Jesus Christ His Son, and in the ultimate worth and lofty destiny of man. But religion in a general sense cannot be equated with our own or indeed with any one set of ideals.

There is also the further difficulty that religionists may be not unreasonably afraid that too cool a scrutiny may diminish the value of what they hold dear or tarnish their feeling towards it. And indeed there is a difference between the mental attitudes of the student and the worshipper. The worshipper is—must be—constrained by loyalty, faith, and awe. The obligation of the student is to truth; yet in the pursuit of truth he is surely required to control and use, rather than divest himself of, all feeling and emotion. Hence the attitudes of student and of worshipper are within the compass of a single individual.

Nonreligionists, too, may find it difficult to give sufficient weight to phenomena which they judge to have no ultimate objective validity, to be no more than stupendous projections of the human imagination. Thus religionists and nonreligionists alike may find it difficult to examine the part played by religion in society without ethnocentrism and without bias.

These are real problems. Nevertheless scholars who hold the most diverse opinions about the empirical (that is, experimentally verifiable in terms of natural science) reality of "things unseen" are increasingly in agreement about the very real and practical significance of nonempirical (that is, incapable of verification by experimental methods) things in social life. It is not that they misunderstand the nature of the truths or the techniques established by the natural sciences, but that they are also aware (as are many natural scientists themselves) that the truths of natural science are not the only kind of truths men live by. Indeed, science itself, as it is conceived by many, is not merely a bundle of techniques, of means adapted to ends, but a faith—a faith in the eventual power of human reason to understand and control the universe.

Many sociologists now attempt to define religion from the standpoint of man as an actor, and they place special emphasis on the way he uses religion in his social life, and indeed, in his total life situation. Though the older attempts to define religion in terms of its origins have been largely given up as hopeless, the newer point of view, though less dogmatic, involves certain more or less explicit assumptions about man himself, his nature, and his needs. This exploration for the motivation of religion belongs, perhaps, more to social psychology than to sociology proper.

Older writers like Tylor and Spencer thought of religion as an outcome of man's reason and his need to know. This is part, but not all, of the truth. Durkheim, and later Freud, stressed the instinctual and emotional bases of religion. But though feeling and emotion are aspects of religious behavior, religion itself cannot be written off as "nothing but" the outcome of crowd excitement (as Durkheim at times called it) or, as with Freud, of sublimated sexual drives. Alone among the animals man is capable of symbolic language and abstract thought. He does not only act and re-act, but innovates and anticipates action. Therefore, as Walt Whitman once observed, man is nature's only worrier; Whitman had a poet's perception that man's need to come to terms with his anxiety was somehow connected with his inveterate religiousness.

Modern social research has done much to confirm Whitman's insight. But man does not anticipate the future with anxiety only. His power to anticipate acts also as a spur to his creative imagination, his yearning, and his hope. In addition we find man not only experiencing but reflecting on his experiences and struggling to create interpretations which will make sense of his experiences.

Man's religion, unlike his economy, cannot be derived from any one of the endowments that he shares with other animals. Nor can it be thought of as stemming from any one aspect of his distinctively human attributes. However significant for religion the long period of dependency of the human young on their parents may be, neither God nor gods can be explained as nothing but a massive projection or projections of parental images. Such theories may afford us partial insights, but no simple explanation is adequate. Modern social science points to the fact that the motivation for religion is as complex as human conditions themselves.

We have, of course, not solved the problem of the motivation of religion. But we have indicated at least some aspects of the total human situation in which religion is embedded as a preliminary to undertaking an analysis of religious behavior and its relationship to society.

All that we have said so far is implied in the statement that religion is a product of culture, an outgrowth of man's activity as a culture-bearing creature. From the point of view of the sociologist, then, religion may be regarded as a cultural tool by means of which man has been able to accommodate himself to his experiences in his total environment; the latter includes himself, his fellow group members, the world of nature, and that which is felt by him to transcend them all. It is this last—the direction of human thought, feeling, and action to things which man feels to be beyond his ordinary everyday experiences with himself, his fellows, and the natural world, that is, the *sacred*—that constitutes, we believe, the very core of religion.

The Meaning of the Sacred

What then is the sacred?[2] It is something easier by far to recognize than to define. The sacred is concerned with the wonderful and terrible mystery of things. In all known societies there exists a distinction between the holy and the ordinary or, as we often phrase it, the sacred and the secular or profane. Yet there is hardly a thing in heaven or on earth that has not been regarded at some time by some people as sacred. The Hindus revere the Sacred Cow, the Moslems the Black Stone of the Kabah, the Christians the Cross upon the Altar, the Jews the Ark of the Covenant, and many preliterate peoples revere their animal totems (animals believed to symbolize the mythical primal ancestor of the tribe). The things we have just listed are sacred *objects*; they are tangible, concrete. But the sacred has also an unseen, intangible aspect. Sacred *beings* and *entities* of all kinds—gods, spirits, angels, devils, and ghosts—are revered as awesome or holy; the Person of the Risen Christ, the Virgin Mary and the Saints, Zeus and the whole Greek pantheon, entire cosmologies of Buddhas and bodhisattvas, Allah and Mohammed his Prophet are sacred to their respective votaries, and are revered in ceremonials and enshrined in systems of belief.

What common element can we find in this almost infinite variety of sacred objects and entities which we may characterize as the *sacred* itself? If we merely consider the objects and entities in and of themselves, no answer is possible. It is not the things themselves but the nature of the attitudes and the sentiments that reinforce them that is the hallmark of the sacred. Sacredness consists, then, in emotionally supported mental attitudes. Awe itself, the most apparent sacred emotion, is a compound of worship and dread. Awe polarizes the attraction of love and the repulsion of danger. Most emphatically it is not an everyday or secular emotion, but rather a feeling that separates the object or objects to which it is directed from the sphere of the ordinary common sense concerns of everyday. The sacred, then, can be best understood as that which is set apart by the attitude of respect in which it is held from the utilitarian concerns of everyday living; it is that which is not understood by exercise of the empirical common sense that suffices for ordinary practical purposes.

Sacred objects, it should be stressed, are not materially different from ordinary everyday objects. To the uninitiated the Sacred Cow of the Hindus will appear just like any other cow, or the Holy Cross of the Christians like any other two pieces of transfixed wood. Again, it is the attitude of the worshippers that makes the crucial difference. As for the sacred entities or beings, since they are intangible and invisible and thus the reality of their existence cannot be demonstrated experimentally, they may well seem to the uninitiated to be nonexistent. Yet the awe in which they are held by their worshippers is real emotion, and not only invests its objects with their sacred characters, but makes it possible for these "imaginary" entities to exist in the minds of their worshippers. Moreover, such entities, however imaginary, have observable (empirical) consequences.*

Closely allied to the sacred, or the holy, is the unholy, which includes whatever under particular circumstances is thought to desecrate the holy. It is precisely to avoid this possibility of contamination that the sacred is hedged about with prohibitions or taboos. Sacred objects should not be touched or eaten or even closely approached except on special occasions or by specially authorized persons; the name of the sacred being should not be spoken, or if it is, in no ordinary voice or language. The Hebrews, for instance, believe that death awaits the non-Levite who defiles the Ark of the Covenant with his touch; the devout Catholic does not approach the altar on which the consecrated Host lies nearer than a certain distance.

Both Orthodox Jews and Roman Catholics today celebrate the sacred name and the sacred mysteries not in everyday language, but in a special religious language or tongue.

Beliefs and Practices

It is not enough, however, that sacred objects and entities merely "exist"; their existence must be continually renewed and kept alive in the minds of the worshipping group. Beliefs, that is, creeds and myths, and practices, that is, ceremonies and rituals, contribute to this end. Religious belief not only assumes the existence of sacred objects and beings, but by repetition strengthens and reaffirms faith. Belief also attempts to explain the nature and origin of sacred objects and beings, and to provide, so to say, a map and guide to the unseen world. Beliefs may be elaborated into theologies and cosmologies. The theologies may be complicated, highly articulate and intellectualized, such as the Nicene Creed; and the cosmologies may be vast and intricate structures, such as the Hindu cycles of existence or the heaven, purgatory, and inferno of Dante's Christian vision. Or again, they may be simpler and less articulate, such as some preliterate people's beliefs in myths and charms.

Beliefs not only describe and explain sacred beings and the unseen world— God and the angels, Shiva and Krishna, Jupiter and Mars, heaven and hell— but most importantly of all they tell how this world of the unseen is meaningfully related to the actual human world. *Belief* explains how the tangible realities of the bread and wine in the Eucharist are mystically connected with the sacred Body and Blood of the invisible, risen Christ. But whether the belief refers "to the invisible things beyond the senses or to the sacred objects within plain view . . . it is belief based upon faith rather than upon evidence; it is in Biblical language the substance of things hoped for, the evidence of things not seen."[3]

In our thinking about religion we Westerners have, perhaps, tended to put too much stress on belief in its more intellectual aspects, on disputes about theologies and creeds, which have played so important a part in our own reli-

---

* We have no wish to enter into a philosophical discussion here. Our meaning is simply that the things or entities that people believe to exist, whether or not their existence can be empirically demonstrated, actually affect their behavior, and for this reason have observable social results that are independent of their objective existence. One can hold this point of view without prejudging the issue as to whether God—the Ultimate, the Self-Existent— is objectively real.

gious history. For a sociological understanding of religion in general, however, ritual, or ceremonialism, may well be more important. *Ritual* is the active, observable side of religious behavior. It can indeed include any kind of behavior: wearing special clothing, sacrificing life and produce, reciting formulas, maintaining silence, singing, chanting, praying, praising, feasting, fasting, dancing, wailing, washing, reading.[4] Ritual's sacred nature, then, depends, as in the case of sacred objects, not on its intrinsic character, but on the mental and emotional attitudes held by the group towards it and the social and cultural context within which it is performed. The same behavior, eating, for example, may be secular in one context—as when one has breakfast—but sacred in another—as when one partakes of the Host in the celebration of the Mass or shares in the Passover meal. Ritual, in other words, defines the context within which sacred behavior takes place. Ritual also assigns roles to the participants. By regular recurrence and meticulous repetition it channelizes emotion, and so enhances the emotion-evoking power of the symbols used. It is especially effective when people are gathered together, for they stimulate one another. Thus an important function of ritual is to fortify faith in the unseen world and to afford a symbolic means of expression for religious emotion.

Symbolism

Since the essence of religious emotion is viewed as inexpressible, all attempts to express it are approximations and therefore symbolic. Yet as a means of making the unseen world of sacred objects and beings live in the minds and hearts of the worshippers, symbolism, though less exact than more intellectualized modes of expression, has a peculiar potency of its own. Because symbols have a power to evoke feelings and associations over and above mere verbal formulation of the things they are believed to symbolize, they have been throughout history—and they still remain—among the most powerful stimulants of human sentiment. Hence it is not hard to understand that the sharing of common symbols is a particularly effective way of cementing the unity of a group of worshippers here on earth. It is precisely because the referents of symbols elude over-precise intellectual definitions that their unifying force is the more potent; for intellectual definitions make for hair-splitting and divisiveness. Symbols may be shared on the basis of not-too-closely-defined feeling.

The Community of Worshippers

All that we have said so far has implied that the sharing of beliefs and practices by a social group, a group of worshippers, is essential to religion. Only as this sharing takes place can the beliefs and practices be kept alive. The group may be a tribe of Australian aborigines celebrating a totem rite, an assembly of Holy Rollers at a testimonial meeting, a Presbyterian congregation listening devoutly to a sermon, or a quiet gathering of the Religious Society of Friends. The specific form of the rite makes little matter. What does matter is the common sharing.

Human groups who share their beliefs and practices thereby become a *moral community* or, as Durkheim put it, they constitute a "church."[*5] The very

---

* Durkheim did not, of course, mean to imply a church in the narrow sense, that is, an organized church or denomination as we today in the United States understand the term. He was referring to the moral unity of any group of worshippers, whether composed of an entire tribe of people or a more limited group.

process of sharing symbolic rites and beliefs strengthens a group's sense of its own identity, accentuates its "we feeling." This was notably the case among the Australian preliterates who furnished the material for Durkheim's studies, for in sharing the totem meal the worshippers partook of the name of the totem animal and of its very life. But in less direct and dramatic form this strengthening of group identity is a result of all shared worship. Among Moslems the common observance of the hours of public prayer both designates and unites the brotherhood of believers. For many Christians, too, the sharing of a sacramental meal both symbolizes and reaffirms the communion of the faithful.

Moral Values

The sharing of belief and ritual implies that the group members' relationship to the sacred is in some way intimately connected with the group's moral values. This implicit connection is made apparent in the abstention of certain groups of worshippers from particular foods or in the preservation of some particular animal. The cult of the cow was, in the opinion of Gandhi, the one religious value held in common by the entire Hindu world. The cow is, then, a sacred object for the Hindus and their abstention from eating its flesh is a moral value derived from that fact; it serves to unite Hindu worshippers and to distinguish them from beef-eating and non-pork-eating Moslems and Jews. The Jewish dietary laws, assumed to have been enjoined by Yahweh himself, are a classic example of the moral values of a given group being directly traceable to a belief in an immediate divine decree and of their continued observance acting as a most powerful cement of a moral community. In the two cases just cited the connection between the shared moral values of the group and the commands of God or gods in the unseen world is exceedingly clear. The fact is that many distinctive customs of any particular group upon careful analysis are likely to be revealed as stemming from that group's conception of its relation to the sacred; in other words, the customs probably have a religious origin.

This connection between a people's conception of the sacred and the moral values of the group may be illustrated in another way. The kind of relationships that a particular group of human beings believes to exist among the sacred beings in the unseen world, and also between these beings and human kind, is often regarded as the ideal pattern of human relationships that should exist in society itself. For instance, a sheep-herding people may picture their God as the Good Shepherd, and for them the devotion of the good shepherd to his sheep becomes at once the prototype of their God's relationship to them, his worshippers, and also an ideal model for their own relationships to one another. Or again, as with the early Hebrews or the followers of Mohammed, the God may be the prototype of the fierce tribal patriarch who will brook no rival; or, as in Mayahana Buddhism, the heavens may be peopled with benevolent bodhisattvas, the celestial embodiments of magnanimous princes. In these cases the implications for human conduct are apparent. The important issue in this connection is not whether "man creates his gods in his own image," but rather the correspondence between the moral values imputed to the inhabitants of the unseen world and those of their human worshippers. The moral values attributed to the unseen provide a sacred sanction for those of the objective human world.

This interdependency of the moral values of the respective worlds of sacred and human beings is especially significant when the relationships among the former are thought of as kinship relationships. Many religions conceive of the unseen as being peopled by families of sacred beings—families which exemplify widely differing ideals of family life. The example of a sacred family best known to us in the Western world is that described in the Christian Gospels. There are many ways in which the moral values associated with this Holy Family have given a sacred sanction to the values of family life in Western society at large. Equally important for the moral values of Western communities has been the Christian conception of God as the father of all mankind. This ideal of God as Father and the group of worshippers as His children carries with it the implication that all worshippers are, in God, related to one another, and ought to behave towards one another as brothers. In addition, all human authority ought to be patterned on that of a loving father, and justice be tempered with mercy.

In summary we have seen the essential elements of religion to comprise the idea of the sacred, the emotionally charged attitudes associated with the sacred, the beliefs and practices that both express and reinforce these attitudes, and, finally, the sharing of these beliefs and practices by the group of worshippers who represent a community marked by common moral values.[6]

In our definition of religion we have emphasized those aspects which, from the point of view of sociology, are regarded as essentials. We pointed out all along that this definition is applicable to an exceedingly wide and varied range of phenomena. We also indicated common elements in religions that might seem, at first glance, very far removed from one another.

Yet it is more than likely that we have, in the opinion of some readers, omitted what is for them the very spirit and essence of religion. Some of these omissions and inadequacies are inherent in any attempt to understand anything so exceedingly complex as religion in terms of the approach of any single discipline. Such an attempt is worth while, however, if it helps us to become aware of certain aspects of religion and religious behavior that may previously have escaped our notice, and if it also provides us with a basis for the interpretation of what we are thus enabled to observe.*

At this point we ask the reader to make a careful note of his objections and queries and file them for future reference. We also ask him to keep a thumb in these pages because we certainly did not insert the preceding paragraphs "just for the fun of it," much less to do obeisance to the great god of academic respectability, but we shall be referring to them many times in the pages that follow.

If as he went along the reader has been mentally trying on our definition for size and comparing it with his own religious experiences, in certain respects the fit should have been easy. He probably recognized rather readily certain tenets of his church as beliefs, and appreciated the *sacred* character of such of them as his church deemed it inappropriate to subject to empirical or scientific proof. Similarly, in connection with the rituals or practices, the reader probably thought of some, at any rate, which he considers as "set apart by an attitude of special respect" from the utilitarian affairs of everyday. He might have recognized, too, that the creeds and rituals characteristic of his particular reli-

---

* For a clear account of this role of concepts in sociological study see Ely Chinoy: *Sociological Perspective: Basic Concepts and Their Application* (Studies in Sociology) New York, Random House, Inc., 1954, especially Chap. One.

gious community are known and felt emotionally, in a kind of expressive short-hand, by means of symbols. Among such symbols and symbolic acts are the cross on the Christian altar and the lighting of the candles in an Orthodox Jewish home on Friday night. These symbols are capable of invoking in the minds of the worshippers almost instantaneously a whole network of memories and sentiments. These associations activate and intensify the shared loyalties of the group members and make them more keenly aware of their differences from other groups.

We think the reader will also have been conscious of some of the constraints, more or less strong depending on himself and the religious community under consideration, upon the members to live up to the moral values stressed by his particular church. Whatever these moral values may be—and they concern a wide range of activities—the emphasis which a religious group places on particular values makes this group distinctive from others. Since these values are stressed by ministers, priests, and rabbis and impressed by parents on their children from one generation to another, the reader will understand how adherence to such values serves to weld the group of worshippers into a moral community.

The Sacred and the Supernatural

It would not surprise the author, however, if the reader finds some trouble in coming to grips with the interpretation we have given to the term sacred. If, as we have claimed, the sacred is vital to religion, the reader may wish to know, for example, whether our concept of the sacred includes the supernatural or not, or whether the sacred is identical with the supernatural, or further, whether a religion can exist without a supernatural basis? If such questions have occurred to the reader he will have put his finger on some of the most controversial issues among students of religion.

The sacred, as we defined it earlier, includes the supernatural but is not identical with it. Since, as we explained, sacredness inheres in the attitudes of the worshippers, the referents of the attitudes may be objects and entities in this world (regarded in a special way) or objects and entities in the supernatural world. The supernatural, in contrast to the sacred, may be thought of as comprising only other-worldly objects and entities which are assumed to transcend the empirically known world.* In most Christian and Jewish denominations, and indeed in most of the great spiritual religions of the world, the supernatural in this sense is the main object of religious attitudes. Natural objects as symbols, however, are also regarded in a sacred way. In the supernatural world God and heaven are sacred; in the natural world there are sacred books and candles: symbols, for the most part, of supernatural things.

We become involved in deeper problems, however, if we raise the further question: "Is a religion really a religion if the objects and entities regarded by its votaries as sacred consist only of natural, this-worldly objects and entities?" In other words, suppose the supernatural point of reference for attitudes of respect and awe associated with the sacred is entirely lacking? And what kind

---

* The term supernatural is sometimes understood by different people in different ways. To some the supernatural appears mainly as a contradiction of nature or indeed as a violation of nature. We have, however, limited our interpretation of the term supernatural to that which is regarded as above and beyond the natural world, and not necessarily in contradiction to it.

of religions are possible if attitudes of reverence and respect are bestowed only on this-worldly objects and beings? These questions, especially today, are not merely academic.

Supernatural and Secular Religions

The traditional world religions of Buddhism, Judaism, Christianity, Hinduism, and Islam, with their emphasis on sacred, other-worldly values, are all religions of the supernatural. There are, however, powerful movements in the modern world which do not emphasize supernaturalism and yet possess most of the other characteristics of religions. These movements have their beliefs and rituals, their symbolism, their groups of devoted adherents bound together by shared moral values. We refer, of course, to the great world movements of nationalism, socialism, fascism, and communism. The sacred focus of these movements, if sacred attitudes may be thought to obtain at all, is on human life in this world, on particular national communities, or on theories in regard to the conduct of human societies. Since supernatural values are missing, should we exclude such movements from the category of religions? Some students who hold that the supernatural is the essence of religion would say that we should. The author, who has accepted the more inclusive category of the sacred, would prefer to classify such movements as nonsupernatural or secular religions.

Consider the case of communism. Communist theory professes a materialistic view of society and, indeed, of the universe. Far from regarding supernatural entities with respect and awe, communists until recently severely restricted the practice of supernatural religion and had their museums dedicated to atheism and scientific materialism. There is no basis for a supernatural religion here. But if we ask ourselves whether or not communists regard certain phenomena as sacred, the answer we must give is different. For there are things they regard with an attitude of much more than everyday respect, entities which some of them at least view with awe, not what is known as common sense.

There would be nothing sacred about communism if communists were concerned only with achieving practical ends with the practical means appropriate to such achievement. But communism is also a faith—faith in the Marxian dialectic as something that will work itself out and produce a classless society—a kind of heaven on earth, supposedly—independently of or even in spite of the political and economic means used. Many communists have worked and suffered and died for this faith. Looked at in this way, as a faith in an unverifiable historical principle, communism is a religion, though not a supernatural one. Regarded purely from the standpoint of a political power structure, of course, there is nothing distinctively religious about communism.

Consider nationalism in a similar way. A national group organized for purposes of protection and the good life is not in itself a sacred phenomenon. Nationalism takes on a sacred aspect, however, when a mystical attitude towards the nation as an entity takes the place of a common-sense regard for the well-being of the members for whom the organized group exists.

It may seem to some a remarkable fact that in spite of the decline in the hold of supernatural religions on many people in recent times all over the world, religious attitudes still persist. These attitudes it seems can be readily redirected to nonsupernatural values—to the nation, to the state, or to man-made, so-called scientific theories such as Marxism. It appears that religion as well as nature abhors a vacuum. Indeed, the increasingly dynamic character of what we have called the secular religions of the modern world is eloquent testimony to that universality of religion among human kind that we mentioned at the outset. This fact of its universality in turn raises important questions about religion's function in human societies. These questions are the theme of the following chapter.

Footnotes to Chapter One

1. James, William: *The Varieties of Religious Experience*, New York, Modern Library, Inc., 1937, pp. 31–2.
2. Cf. Durkheim, Émile: *The Elementary Forms of the Religious Life*, Translated by J. W. Swain, Glencoe, Ill., The Free Press, 1947, pp. 37–42.
3. Davis, Kingsley: *Human Society*, New York, The Macmillan Company, 1949, p. 534.
4. *Ibid.*, p. 534.
5. Durkheim, Émile: *op. cit.*, pp. 43–4.
6. *Ibid.*, p. 47.

chapter two

Functions of Religion in Human Societies

Religion and the Functional Approach

As students of sociology our main concern with religion, as we pointed out at the start, is with its function in human society. The term *function*, we noted, refers to the contribution of religion, or of any other social institution, to the maintenance of human societies as going concerns. Our interest, then, is in the part that religion has played and still plays in furthering their survival. Sociologists are of course also interested in analyzing different types of religious organization, in various types of leadership and followership, and in the interconnections between religious institutions and the other institutions of society. They are also interested in certain features of religious organization peculiar to the American scene, and in a more general way in understanding and accounting for some of the consistencies and similarities between the religious culture and the broader culture of particular societies. All these aspects of religion will come in for some discussion in this study. They are, however, subsidiary to the basic problem of religion's functions which is the concern of this chapter.

In attempting to analyze the social functions of religious behavior we must be careful to distinguish between what people, the members of any particular group of worshippers, intend to achieve by their behavior and the unintended effect of this behavior in social life.[1] If we were to ask a Tibetan devotee why he repeatedly turned his prayer wheel and chanted "Om padme Om," or interrogated a "shouting" Methodist as to the reason for his ebullient enthusiasm, their answers would be very unlikely to show that they had any particular intentions in regard to society at all. The intended effect of the Tibetan's action is to further his attainment of the bliss of Nirvana, and that of the Methodist's to give vent to his happy knowledge that he is saved by grace from his sins. They, in common with many other practitioners of religions, are deeply concerned with the attainment of certain states of consciousness. Other avowed objectives of members of various religious groups are connected with the life in other worlds, with the gaining of heaven and the avoidance of hell, with the mitigation of the lot of souls in purgatory, and with the securing of one's transmigration into a superior type of being. Still other religious votaries may say that their aim is to bring their spirits into harmony with the universe, or to glorify God and perform His will more perfectly, or by prayer to prevail upon the gods to bestow benefits upon human beings.

Without some such conscious intentions the religious behavior would most probably not be performed. Indeed, it is entirely without prejudice against the intentions of the worshippers that the sociologist maintains that the unin-

12

tended consequences of their behavior are often of greater importance for the maintenance of societies than their conscious aims.* Individuals are, of course, sometimes conscious of social purposes of their membership in religious groups. Such purposes, however, are apt to be regarded by the groups' members as subsidiary and subordinate to their main religious function. Yet the fact that people are themselves more often than not unaware of many of the social effects of their religious behavior in no way minimizes its impact.

Religion's Contribution to the Maintenance of Societies

What, then, are the essential requirements for the survival of human societies, and what contribution does religion make to them? Before we attempt to answer this question we should make clear the limits of the context within which we are about to consider it. We shall be satisfied if we can show first that societies have certain minimal survival and maintenance needs, and second that religion functions to fulfil some of them, even though there may be contradictions and discrepancies in the way in which it does so. We do not contend that in all societies and under all circumstances religion (or religion alone) performs this social task, or that religion under all circumstances fulfils all the functions mentioned. With this caution let us examine the organization of society in order to bring out at least some of the minimum essentials for maintaining societies as going concerns.

An American economist once wrote a book with the provocative title *The Promises Men Live By.* For the economist these promises referred to credit. The title was meant to dramatize the fact that the circulation of the lifeblood of an economic system was dependent on whether or not men could count upon one another to meet certain mutual financial obligations. Similarly, societies depend for their survival on the continued expectancy that their members will discharge certain known and acknowledged obligations: in short, that they can be counted upon to honor their social "promises to pay." Furthermore, if there were not some common agreement about the nature and extent of these social obligations, as well as adequate rewards and penalties to ensure their fulfilment, human societies would be in danger of falling apart, like plays in which the actors are perpetually missing their cues.

Thus some degree of common agreement, or *consensus*, about the nature of these crucial obligations, as well as the existence of power sufficient to constrain individuals and groups to fulfill them, is a minimum essential for the persistence of the social order. How, then, is such agreement to be obtained? Again, what constraint is sufficiently strong to induce individuals and groups to forego their self interests for the sake of society as a whole? We will answer these important questions very briefly and then examine our answers more closely.

First, religion has helped to promote agreement about the nature and content of social obligations by providing values that serve to channel the attitudes of a society's members and to define for them the content of their

---

* Unintended functions fulfilled by a particular form of institutional behavior are sometimes referred to by sociologists as *latent* functions; whereas those which represent the intended, the official purposes of the institution are termed *manifest* functions. On this point see especially R. K. Merton: *Social Theory and Social Structure*, Glencoe, Ill., The Free Press, 1949, Chap. I.

social obligations. In this role religion has helped to create systems of social values which are integrated and coherent.

Second, there are good reasons for believing that religion has also played a vital role in supplying the constraining power that underwrites and reinforces custom. In this connection it should be noted that the attitudes of reverence and respect with which especially binding customs (*mores*) are regarded are closely akin to the feelings of awe which, as we saw earlier, are evoked by the sacred itself.

Religion and the Integration of Values

It has always been difficult for human beings to agree for any appreciable length of time to regulate their behavior in terms of a miscellaneous conglomeration of unrelated prohibitions and commands. Many a disciplinary crisis in prison, army, or school life has shown that group consensus tends to break down when discipline is experienced as completely arbitrary, unprincipled, and therefore meaningless. In such crises groups may be held in line by the use of physical force. History bears witness, however, that human societies cannot be maintained for long periods by the exercise of physical force alone.

If human societies are to remain stable, and if man's social conduct is to be reasonably orderly and predictable, considerable behavior must be channeled and patterned in accordance with certain rather well-understood and self-consistent principles. These principles are related to the goals or focal points of men's social behavior. Such goals are commonly referred to by sociologists as *values*.* It is only when the values of a society are themselves integrated into a meaningful whole, or system, that the society's members can be in agreement as to the direction of their behavior (a condition probably never reached in full).

Religion has accounted in large part for the fact that values in almost all human societies are not a mere hodge-podge but constitute a hierarchy. In this hierarchy religion defines the *ultimate* values. Ultimate values, with their implications for conduct, derive their meaning, as we pointed out earlier, from the kind of relationship the group believes to exist between its members and their deities or other objects of religious faith. For instance, if God, as an ultimate value, is conceived of as a loving father, the content of this higher value has a direct bearing on the content of intermediate and subordinate values in the entire value-hierarchy. Important among the intermediate values are values placed by members of a society upon one another and also upon material objects such as money or land. Thus, by reason of its definition of the highest values, religion has coordinated (often unknowingly) into more or less integrated systems numerous diverse values that might overwise appear

---

* We can perhaps understand more clearly how religion has helped to bring about that minimal consensus essential for the on-going of societies if we undertand how social attitudes are related to social values. When sociologists speak of the attitudes of the members of any society, they use the term *attitude* to designate *habitual tendencies to act in particular ways towards particular objects*. It is thus the objects, the goals, of social attitudes that are invested with social values. In consequence the values (objects of social attitudes) may refer to concrete things, such as money or land, or to concrete beings such as a sweetheart or a child. But values may also refer to abstractions, such as some sacred entity or god, or to some customary way of fulfilling social obligations, as, for instance, paying respect to parents, honoring debts, or regulating sexual behavior. Thus the values of a given society inhere in a great variety of phenomena.

as unrelated and meaningless. Furthermore this integration of values, by making them appear more understandable, also increases the chances of consensus in regard to them.

Religion and the Reinforcement of Values

If we could forget screaming newspaper headlines and think instead about the behavior of the vast majority of ordinary folks, we might be surprised by the fact that most people in most societies actually do fulfil their social obligations most of the time. Why is this? One explanation that readily comes to mind is force of habit—the constraining power of sheer custom backed by human inertia. This explanation tells us part of the story but also leaves much unaccounted for. It serves to raise the further question: What gives custom its constraining power? For it is one thing for societies to invest with value the most important goals of social activity; but it is quite another thing for the habitual behavior of the members to be generally in accord with those values. In all societies, however, more or less clear notions of appropriate behavior are found. These ideal standards of behavior—these "oughts"—which incorporate social values, are often referred to by sociologists as *social norms*.

The very existence of such norms (important among which are religious norms) makes behavior in conformity with them probable. But such conformity is even more likely when norms are buttressed by potent rewards and punishments. Social rewards and punishments (or sanctions) are, to be sure, implicit to some degree in all social norms, if only because most human beings feel rewarded psychologically when they conform to what is expected of them and experience as punishment the informal—as well as the legal—censure of their fellows. When norms occur in a sacred frame of reference, however, they are backed up by sacred sanctions, and in almost all societies sacred sanctions have a special constraining force. For not only human, this-worldly rewards and punishments are involved, but suprahuman, other-worldly prizes and penalties as well.

The work of Durkheim has done more than that of any other single sociologist to throw light on the nature of this interaction between social values and related norms and the habitual fulfilment of social and moral obligations by most members of human societies. To Durkheim, indeed, the most significant property of the sacred itself was its capacity to evoke awe, and hence its constraining power over human behavior and its consequent reinforcement of the moral values of the worshipping group. It is true that Durkheim, in his quest for a common point of reference for sacred attitudes and emotions (which may be directed, as we have seen already, to an infinite variety of objects and entities), was led to formulate the bold hypothesis that all these objects and entities are but symbols of a single underlying moral entity to which the real, though possibly unconscious, reverence and awe of human beings are directed. This basic entity was thought by Durkheim to be society.

This hypothesis in which Durkheim held that all objects and entities invested by men with sacred quality are fundamentally symbols of the human group itself, making society the ultimate object of human worpship,[2] has been repugnant to all religionists and is also regarded by most sociologists as unacceptable for a variety of reasons—including the reason that it is unverifiable. Yet, like many great but mistaken hypotheses, this view of Durkheim's has opened up many new insights. Even if we reject it in the form in which it is stated, it may still suggest to us important clues concerning the moral nature of the constraint that human societies exercise over the behavior of their members. In particular the steps by which Durkheim arrived at his conclusions may help to illuminate our present discussion; for his stress on the awe-compelling properties of the sacred and his perception of the nature of its constraining power suggest some of the significant ways in which sacred sanctions reinforce society's values.

The Social Role of Religion: Some Conclusions and Questions

The social role of religion is thus seen to be, in the main, an integrative one. In the literal sense of the word, religion promotes a binding together, both of the members of societies and of the social obligations that help to unite them. Since the values underlying systems of social obligation are shared by religious groups, religion secures for the society a large measure of common agreement. Religion also tends to conserve social values. The very fact that religious values are sacred means that they are not easily changed in response to changes involving secular conceptions of utility and convenience.

Although religion has a role in society as an integrative and cohesive and also conservative force, it functions in other ways as well.[3] Indeed, the very fact that a religion so powerfully binds together its own group of worshippers means that if a religion is not shared by all or most members of a society, it may be a sharply divisive and disruptive, even a destructive, force. Furthermore, religion does not invariably play a conservative, stabilizing role. Particularly in times of cataclysmic social and economic change religion has often played a creative, innovating—even revolutionary—part.

We do not get very far in our analysis when we attempt to characterize the functions of religion in a social vacuum. For the degree to which religion has had integrating and conservative functions, or the extent to which it has fostered either divisiveness or creative innovation, has varied markedly at different historical periods and in societies of different types. Thus since discussion of the varying social functions of religion in abstract general terms has limited meaning, we propose in Chapter Three to consider the role religion plays in three different types of society.

The evaluation of the role of religion in society raises a basic problem we can do little more than mention here. We said at the outset that our main concern is the part played by religion in furthering—or hampering—the survival and maintenance of human groups. Granted that a undefined minimum of integration, cohesion, and stability is essential for the maintenance of all societies at all times, we are still left with the task of assessing how much integration or stability is in fact required to preserve different societies under different sets of circumstances. Furthermore, in this context the term *maintain* is ambiguous, for societies may persist in greater or lesser degrees of social health. It would appear that too much conservatism or even too much integration may in some societies serve a negative rather than a positive social function, in other words, be dysfunctional. But again, how much integration, innovation, or stability is too much? These are exceedingly difficult questions to which no completely objective answers can be given. Individual judgments of value are inescapably involved, and such judgments are bound to differ. We propose, however, to outline some of the pertinent aspects of the relationship between religion and human societies on which these judgments of value are characteristically based.

Finally, religions and religious values do not affect societies as purely external forces which set their imprint upon human beings from the outside, as it were. Religious values play a role in society only in so far as they are learned, appropriated, and internalized by the individual members. The fact that instruction in religious values forms a large part of the explicit or implicit training of children in all societies and that this instruction takes place at a time when the personal values of the individuals are being formed, guarantees at least some degree of consistency between individual values and religious values.

Religion and Socialization of the Individual

A necessary counterpart, then, to the integrating role of religion is its functional contribution to the socialization of the individual members of societies. Each individual as he grows up needs a system of values as a kind of general guide for his activity in society, and to serve as an integrating focus for his developing personality. Parents pass on to their children, though often informally or unconsciously, their society's system of values, with of course certain personal modifications of their own. Since in almost all societies religious values have a high priority—they furnish the ultimate sanctions for relationships between parent and child, brother and sister, husband and wife, buyer and seller—these values are taught to children in their most impressionable years. The values that a person learns at his mother's knee are the ones that are most deeply imbedded in his personality; this fact explains in part why he is vulnerable to parental suggestion. Moreover, no society allows parents to shirk entirely the duty of "moralizing" their children, for their indoctrination in the values of the society is essential for the maintenance of the society itself in the generation to come.

Since religious values form the keystone of most systems of social values, the most important lessons that children learn are in the field of what we today often call *religious education*. Throughout most of the world religious education, broadly conceived, helps the individual to make sense of much instruction which might otherwise appear to him as a meaningless and arbitrary assortment of directions and prohibitions. If, for instance, a child learns (as in some Christian denominations) that the attainment of salvation is the main goal of life and that to that end he is to attend church regularly, read the Bible and pray daily, honor and love his parents, work hard, live frugally, refrain from dishonest conduct, unchastity and riotous behavior, avoid dancing, drinking and card-playing, his social development is not only given a very definite direction but a certain internal consistency. Moreover his choice of immediate goals becomes almost predetermined.

Such a rigid integration of an individual's life in accordance with the values of evangelical Christianity is very rare in our modern big-city life, though much less rare, even today in the United States, in rural areas, particularly in the South. Personality integration rooted primarily in the internalization of religious values is common, however, in vast areas of the world where a relatively isolated type of village life prevails. In our complex American society, in which many people shift from country to city life an early integration of a person's life around religious values may sometimes become a source of great conflict for him, especially if in later life he is exposed to the influence not only of other religious faiths but of the pervasive impact of a highly secularized society. Such conflict may also be the lot of individuals in widely scattered parts of the world, who, without education or preparation, are brought into sudden contact with Western secular values. These comments about the possibly divisive as well as integrating role of religion in personality development suggest that here too we will need to consider variations in the functions of religion in different types of societies.

Before discussing these differences, however, there is another general aspect of the part played by religion in the integration of personality that should be brought out. The ultimate goals of religion are nontangible. Whether the Buddhist's Nirvana, the Christian's salvation, or the Moslem's heaven of eternal delights, they lie in another, unseen world. This fact has at least two important consequences for the personality. In most societies success in this world is a goal attainable only by a few. Other-worldly goals are open equally to all.[4] Again, success in this world is open to observation and is subject to check by everyday methods of reckoning. But achievement of other-worldly success is invisible, and may be known only to a select group of initiates, or possibly only in the heart of the individual himself.

Therefore the person who is a failure by the standards of the secular world may, because of his internalization of religious values, be better able to accept and explain to himself this lack of secular achievement without risk of personality disintegration. Indeed, if religious values are paramount with him, no lack of success in this world need be interpreted as absolute. The financial or social failure may still aspire to sainthood, the sick and unfortunate may still strive for salvation. Important avenues to happiness and fulfillment still remain open.

From this situation society itself is indirectly the gainer, for its individual members are thus fortified and encouraged not only to continue their pursuit of religious goals but also to continue undismayed to play their part in keeping up the system of social obligations on which the stability of society depends.

Footnotes to Chapter Two

1. Cf. Merton, Robert K.: *Social Theory and Social Structure*, Glencoe, Ill., The Free Press, 1949, pp. 61–4.
2. Durkheim, Émile: *The Elementary Forms of the Religious Life*, Glencoe, Ill., The Free Press, 1949, pp. 206–7.
3. Merton, Robert K.: *op. cit.*, pp. 30–2.
4. Cf. Davis, Kingsley: *Human Society*, New York, The Macmillan Company, 1949, p. 532.

chapter three

Types of Society and Religion

Why Types of Society?

In all societies, as we have stressed, people distinguish between sacred and secular concerns. Yet societies vary enormously in the degree to which they emphasize the sacred values. In some societies the sacred is an aspect of almost all behavior; in others, such as our own, more and more human values are regarded as secular and are subject to the valuations of utility and common sense. In modern society the area of operation of the sacred is pushed back, delimited, and labeled. We cannot understand the functions of religion in any specific society unless we have at least some grasp of general variations in the over-all organization of societies and corresponding variations in the organization of religion itself.

There are many subtle shadings of difference in the degree of secularization as well as in the manner of organization of concrete societies; to describe them all is impossible. But we can depict certain general variations. Thus in the pages which follow we present synthetic, thumbnail descriptions of three types of societies.[1] Type one is a society in which sacred values predominate. Type three is a society in which secular values are in the ascendancy. Type two represents a kind of way station between the other two types.[2]

No one of the descriptions which follow represents an actual society in its entirety. In fact, in each case we have purposely exaggerated certain features and all our descriptions are of necessity oversimplified. Nor do these three types represent inevitable stages of historical development, though many but by no means all societies have passed or are passing through these or similar stages. Yet approximations to these types of society have existed in historical times and may also be found today—sometimes in uneasy proximity—in our rapidly shrinking world. The usefulness of these descriptions for the reader will consist in their availability as yardsticks, so that he may check against them the concrete characteristics of the societies he encounters either at first hand or in the pages of books.

The reader will observe that in addition to describing the organizational features of these types of societies and of their religious systems we are concerned with the extent to which religion has or has not played an integrating role both in the different societal types as total entities and in the personalities of their individual members.

Type One: Preliterate Societies and Sacred Values

Societies representing our first type are characteristically small, isolated, and preliterate.[3] They have a low level of technical development and relatively little division of labor or elaboration of social classes. The family is their most

19

important institution and specialization of the organization of governmental and economic life is rudimentary. The rate of social change is slow.

Every member of this type of society shares the religion of the total group; thus membership in the society and in the religious group are synonymous. Religious organization itself constitutes not so much a separate institution as an aspect of the total activities of the group. Religion pervades other group activities, whether economic, political, familial, or recreational. For example, the Trobriand islanders, those South Sea islanders made known to us through the famous researches of the anthropologist Malinowski, build their canoes and plant their gardens (economic and technical operations) as part and parcel of their performance of magical and religious rituals that traditionally accompany the jobs.

This type of society is sufficiently small in size for most of its customs to be known, at least by hearsay, to all its members. It follows that, first, religion is in a position to place its sacred imprint on the value system of the society in a total way; second, in the relatively undeveloped state of the other institutions, except the family, religion is likely to provide the principal focus for the integration and cohesion of the society as a whole. Religious values, as we have seen, often promote conservatism and militate against change; this is an important reason why the hand of tradition is heavy in such societies. Again, because of the absence of rival interests and the fusion of religion with almost all aspects of social life, religion exercises a dominantly cohesive, stabilizing influence.

For the individual, religion puts its stamp on the entire socialization process. Socialization is marked by religious rituals at birth, puberty, marriage, and other crucial times in the life cycle. Personality organization is closely related to religious values, which are handed on directly to the developing person by family and community. In the absence of a variety of possibly competing personality models, especially secular models, religion stands unrivaled as an integrating focus for the personality patterning of individuals in societies of this type.*

This mode of life, which we have called type one, represents the kind of society that anthropologists have studied for many years. Anthropologists have enormously helped the sociologists in the latters' investigation of religion—even of modern religion—with analyses of the functions of religion in relatively simple societies where the bones, so to say, of social structure are less obscured by complex developments. Anthropologists have also drawn our attention to continuing aspects of religious functions in more complex societies that otherwise probably would have been overlooked. Nonetheless more complex social conditions are associated with important modifications in the role played by religion. These modifications are revealed in considering societies of type two.

Type Two: Changing Preindustrial Societies

Societies of type two are less isolated, change more rapidly, are larger in both area and population, and are marked by a higher degree of technological

---

* This type of society especially, perhaps, gives rise to the "tradition-directed" character type, to use David Riesman's popular terms. See his provocative sociological essay, The Lonely Crowd, New Haven, Yale University Press, 1950, Chap. I.(Reprinted as an Anchor Book, 1954.)

development than societies of type one. Considerable division of labor, distinctiveness and diversity of social classes, and some degree of literacy are common features. Agriculture and hand industries are the chief means of support of a village economy, with a few urban trading centers. The institutions of government and economic life are becoming specialized and distinct. Though there is more overlapping of governmental, economic, religious, familial, and recreational activities than in modern industrialized societies (to be considered below as type three), sharper lines are drawn between the occasions on which people go to work, go to play, or go to worship than, say, among the Trobrianders.

A single religious organization which commonly includes all the members characterizes this type of society, yet it is a separate, distinct, and formal organization with its own professional personnel. The institution of government is in the process of development and is a potential rival of religious organization, that is, the church, as a focus for the cohesion, integration, and stabilization of the society. Yet government in such a society is often not sufficiently secularized to be able to dispense with a sacred endorsement for its authority. Though the organizations of religion and government are typically distinct, secular rulers are apt to claim a sacred status, possibly as emperor-gods or royal priests. The Holy Roman Emperors of the medieval West, for example, made sure of their sacred sanction by being anointed by the Popes.

(Religion gives meaning and cohesion to the value system of this type of society, to be sure, but at the same time the spheres of the sacred and the secular are more or less distinguishable. Nevertheless, many phases of social life, for example, of family and economic activities, and the regular recurrence of the seasons, are ritual-laden. The approved patterns for all major social roles—man, woman, husband, wife, parent, child, ruler, ruled, buyer, seller, landlord, tenant, warrior, priest, scholar—receive the sanction of religion. On the other hand, religion does not furnish so complete an endorsement of daily activities as in societies of type one. Moreover, religious belief itself is apt to be fairly well developed as a self-contained system. Religion, as in societies of type one, is not merely an aspect and hence an implicit endorsement of custom, but constitutes to some extent a rival system of sanctioned behavior. Religion is assumed to be of universal application and is thought of as being "higher" than the everyday standards of ordinary social life. The excoriation of the prevailing customs of Israel and Judah by the Hebrew prophets Amos and Hosea because they fell short of religious standards furnishes a dramatic example of this disparity between religious ethic and social custom as conceived of in societies of this type)

Here, then, is a possibility of tension between a religious value system and the society as a whole, though the tendency for religion to become resubmerged in social tradition remains. However, in type two societies religion is potentially a focus for both creative innovation and for social disruption. It is worth noting in this connection that the great "founded" ethical religions of the world—Buddhism, Prophetic Judaism, Christianity, and Islam—had their origin and grew to maturity in societies of this type.

By now it should be clear that religion has other than integrating functions in this type of society. Why is this the case? In the first place, such a society is typically an expanding one. In it the coupling of religious organization (claiming to be the repository of a universal ethic) with the political power structure provides a setting in which attempts to spread the religion become fused with efforts to extend political domination. This situation has bred great religious-political clashes between societies. Such clashes may be regarded as integrating in that they have served to weld together the respective societies involved. From this point of view the Crusades may be said to have helped to integrate Western Christendom. But on the larger stage the bloody wars between Christianity and Islam are important examples of religion's disruptive and destructive tendencies; and even within Christendom itself it may be argued that the Crusades unleashed disintegrating forces at least as potent as those which they harnessed.

In the second place, in the later stages of the development of this type of society, conflicts of interests between religious and political organizations usually arise. These conflicts become acute to the degree, it seems, in which each organization develops its own hierarchical structure and rationale. Each on its own level makes a total claim on the loyalty of the individual members of the society. Since religious organization always has a this-worldly as well as an other-worldly point of reference, and therefore its operations cannot be kept altogether distinct from those of the political authority, divisions and conflicts are bound to occur. The massive church-state struggles in which medieval and early modern Christianity and in which Islam were involved are instances of such occurrences.

In the third place, as societies of type two become increasingly complex and the dominant classes of an earlier period begin to yield ground before the challenge of rising classes representing a newly emergent political and economic order, religion may be a source of creative innovations. Such innovations may be temporarily disintegrating, but in the long run often contribute to the integration of a different type of society, as we shall illustrate shortly.

Religious values in societies of type two furnish the main focus for the integration of the individual's behavior and the formation of his self-image. The fact that most of the members of the society are also members of a single dominant religious organization, which as a rule also controls the tools of literacy and education, lessens the likelihood of internal psychic conflicts on religious grounds. And also the sacred sanction given by the church to the system of statuses and vocations current in the society makes it possible for the individual to accept his social station with a minimum of internal conflict.* With the passage of time in such a society, however, both the increase in literacy and contact with other cultures encourage religious heresy and scepticism. Societies of this type have produced an Arius, an Averroës, and an Abelard among their dissenters.

Our description of this second type of society necessarily has been formulated in dynamic terms. The process of change that marks this type becomes increasingly apparent as such societies evolve. Not only do economic and technological developments play an indispensable part in breaking the "cake of custom," but internal developments within religion itself, in its beliefs, practices, and social organization, also contribute importantly to this end. An even greater acceleration of the tempo of change characterizes societies of type three.

---

* Here, it may be surmised, is an important source of Riesman's "inner-directed" (or gyroscopically governed) character type.

Type Three: Industrial-Secular Societies

There are a number of subtypes within the type three class of societies[4] which our typology cannot adequately take into account. The description below is no doubt somewhat slanted towards modern United States urban society. The latter, however, because of its high degree of secularism, may be regarded as one of the nearest approximations to societies of our type three.

These societies are highly dynamic. Technology increasingly affects all aspects of life, most immediately adjustments to the physical universe, but as significantly human relationships themselves. The influence of science and technology upon society also has important consequences for religion. For this influence is one reason why members of these societies become more and more accustomed to apply methods of empirical common sense and efficiency to more and more human concerns. Thus the sphere of the secular is being continually enlarged—often at the expense of that of the sacred. In large part this secularizing trend accounts for the fact that religious beliefs and practices are confined to smaller and more specialized segments of the life of the society and its members. To keep pace with this trend and in order to retain their influence the churches themselves engage in a growing number of secular activities. In spite of the efforts of some churches to compete with secular institutions the trend continues to relegate religion to limited times and places. In this respect the contrast with societies of type one in which religion is an aspect of most social activity is vivid.

In modern complex societies religious organization is divided and pluralistic. Membership is on a voluntary basis, at least in principle. No single dominant church claims, even theoretically, the allegiance of all members of the society, as in the case of societies of type two. With few exceptions no official tie exists between religious organizations and the secular government. In some societies of this type, such as France and the United States, such relationships are legally repudiated; and in countries like England, where there is an official state church, its relation with the government has became attenuated and modified. In general there are a number of competing organizations, large and small, with many members of the society either nonaffiliated or what are termed paper members of churches. For example, in 1950 in the United States about half of the population belonged to no organized religious group.

These characteristics have profound implications for the functions of religion as an integrative or as a disintegrative force in society. Religious divisions combined with the growth of secularism greatly weaken religion's integrating function, and even its divisive power is somewhat blunted. Toleration of religious difference, typical of this kind of society, is partly the outcome of indifference in the face of the growing dominance of the secular value system; religious organizations themselves are not immune to this secularizing influence.

Religious beliefs and practices, however, serve an integrating function within the various organizations themselves. This is particularly apt to be the case when the membership of such groups is largely drawn from class or ethnic minorities within the larger society. Here they fulfil a double duty as centers of "belongingness" for groups deprived or discriminated against in an increas-

ingly depersonalized social order and as possible orientation points for divisive
tendencies.

Assessing the extent of the integrative and value-forming functions of religion and striking a balance between this and its disintegrative potential is a
tricky business. Over against the weakened influence of religious organizations
may be set the fact that the religious values of an earlier day persist in the
society in more or less attenuated form as part of its basic tradition. In this
form the values continue to contribute, to an extent extremely difficult to
measure, to the cohesion of the society. Evidence of this is the frequency,
especially in times of stress, of public appeals to this common heritage of
religious tradition. Presidents open their inaugurals with prayer, and in time
of war or national danger the help of God is solemnly and publicly invoked.

On the other hand, the state and the economic order between them have
taken over important functions performed by religion in societies of types
one and two. For example, the secular sanctions of political law and economic
supply and demand to a large extent underwrite the system of social obligations without which, as we discussed earlier, societies cannot persist. Hence
"How secular can one get?" becomes a vital question. Can the secular institutions do the minimum integrative job essential for society without borrowing back, as it were, some of the reinforcement of the sacred values previously
abandoned?* Various governments in societies of this type have attempted to
reinvest themselves with an aura of the sacred. Whether communist, fascist,
or ultranationalist, they have surrounded themselves with a panoply of quasi-
sacred ritual and claim the total allegiance of the members of the society
not on the common-sense secular grounds of efficient services performed, but
on the quasi-religious ground that the state, as represented by the government
in question, is an end in itself. Such examples give point to our initial query,
though they do not entirely answer it.

The pursuit of economic power may also take on a quasi-sacred tinge. In
many popular descriptions of the economic arrangements of modern societies
it seems at times that the word *money* could be substituted for *moral* without
the reader being made aware of printer's slip or writer's error.

The personalities of relatively few individuals in modern industrial societies
are shaped solely, or even mainly, in accordance with religious values. Weak-
ness of religious values as an integrating focus, of course, is due in part to the
diversity of the value systems of various religious organizations which at times
contend for the individual's loyalty. But the chief rival of all religious value
systems is the increasingly dominant system of secular values. The latter are
clustered around nationalism, science, economic and occupational matters, and
status-striving. In view of these facts, achievement of personality integration is
a more difficult and more self-conscious feat than in societies of types one and
two.

In bringing up their children, however, perhaps the majority of American
parents continue to act as if they regard traditional religious values, or a somewhat modified version of them, as a necessary background for the building of

---

* Another complicating factor is the possibility that societies of this type may be able
to maintain themselves with a looser and somewhat different kind of integration than either
of the previous types discussed. "How much integration is enough?" thus becomes an additional question of significance.

acceptable character. Parents who have themselves long ceased to attend church nevertheless often feel that their children should be taught the elements of a religious faith in Sunday or Sabbath school. A residuum of fear seems to exist among elders that unless they insure a minimum of religious instruction for their children the rising generation may become demoralized and thus unfitted to maintain, as adults, those values that the elders still feel, perhaps inarticulately, to be necessary for the welfare of society. In the United States, where the public school not only takes over much of the socialization job once performed in the family, but also is legally separated from all organized religion, many people who may themselves be members of no church feel that it is neither safe nor fitting for children to be educated in an atmosphere where it may be that the name of God is never mentioned, where no prayer is uttered and no sacred book is read. Thus the practice of many a moral maxim, honored by adults more often in the breach than the observance, is enjoined by the same adults on children and young people. The possibilities of personality conflict here are clear.

There are several prevalent types of adjustment to the problem of personality integration in modern industrial societies. First, the individual's personality may be integrated almost exclusively on the basis of the values of the particular religious organization to which he belongs. This type of integration is probably rather rare today. Second, the individual may frequently achieve a "working" personality integration by a process of compartmentalization. He may combine a more or less conventional acceptance of the so-called Sabbath or Sunday religion with a workaday orientation to secular values. Thus potentially conflicting maxims, such as "love thy neighbor as thyself" and "business is business," are not permitted to come into open collision. Under stress, however, this compartmentalized system may break down, as the case histories of many mental patients attest. In the third type of adjustment some individuals settle for an integration of personality in terms of secular values alone. This mode of adjustment is also rather common, but it too may break down in stress situations such as those involved in warfare. Finally, some people, probably a minority, outstanding among whom are Albert Schweitzer and Alfred North Whitehead, achieve integration in terms of ultimate religious values which they reinterpret and reevaluate in the light of modern philosophy and science. By means of this reinterpretation they bring religious values into what for them (and the author) is a meaningful relationship with modern industrialized societies.

The Intermixture of Types of Society in the Modern World

When we attempt to use the three types of society we have described above as aids in understanding the functions of religion in actual societies, we are at once confronted with a difficulty. No one of these types exists unmixed in any of the great national societies of the modern world. Societies of type three, for instance—the most aggressive and dynamic societies in the world today—are continually impinging with their science, technology, and secular values on the more religiously oriented societies of type two and on the few remaining societies of type one. In comparison, the absence of rapid communication in medieval and early modern times meant that our own Western world experienced a period of relative isolation of several centuries during which took place the transition from a society approximating type two to one more nearly approaching type three. Even so, the accompanying changes in the role of religion in the society did not take place without prolonged and widespread social disintegration and disruption.

Today the great agricultural societies of the world—the modern counterparts of type two—are linked up, whether their members desire it or not, in a world-wide network of rapid communications. Even their agricultural economy has become more and more dependent on world conditions of trade. Moreover, the kind of social life that has developed in the ports and other urban centers in direct contact with the industrialized West does not differ greatly from that of the secularized societies we have designated as type three. Hence the functions of religion in Calcutta, Bombay, Hong Kong, or Singapore are in many respects comparable to the roles it plays in London, Paris, or New York. Yet in the thousands of agricultural villages that make up the greater part of such societies the sacred values of an earlier day remain dominant. Nevertheless, the radio penetrates into all but the most remote of such villages and modern technology is being applied to ancient methods of agriculture. In the societies of type two religious observances and sacred values are intermeshed with traditional agricultural methods and are tied in with long-established patterns of social obligations and relationships. Therefore technological innovations in agriculture and elsewhere cannot fail ultimately to affect the sacred values themselves. When this happens the social functions of religion in these societies will also be modified.

Even in the predominantly industrialized United States there still remain some relatively isolated rural areas, subsocieties in the larger society, where the role played by religion is quite similar to the prevailing situation in societies of type two. The way in which religion serves in large part to define the positions of social ranks in a local community of a somewhat isolated agricultural area in the Midwest was described by James West (pseudonym) in his book *Plainville, U.S.A.* This serves to illustrate the persistent social significance of sacred values in some of our rural areas. The role of religion is different in Plainville than in New York, Chicago, or Los Angeles. Yet these metropolitan cities themselves—our closest approximation to societies of type three—contain many individuals who migrated from either rural areas in the United States or peasant societies of southern and eastern Europe or from Asia, whose values were originally formed in societies similar to those of type two. The expectations of such people concerning the role religion ought to play in social life are apt to be very different from those of most of their urban neighbors.

The existence of these smaller subsocieties within our larger societies with their differing conceptions of religion's role gives rise to conflicts and discrepancies both within the social order and within individual personalities. Some understanding of these conflicts and discrepancies, especially in so far as they result from the close and sometimes enforced contact between societies of different types, is essential for an intelligent grasp of the role of religion in the world today.

Footnotes to Chapter Three

1. Cf. Chinoy, Ely: *Sociological Perspective*, New York, Random House, Inc., 1954, pp. 31-4.

2. For a similar distinction, see Wilson, Logan, and William L. Kolb: *Sociological Analysis*, New York, Harcourt, Brace & Co., 1949, pp. 344–9.
3. Cf. Redfield, Robert: "The Folk Society," *American Journal of Sociology*, January 1947, pp. 293–308.
4. Cf. MacIver, Robert M.: *The Web of Government*, New York, The Macmillan Company, 1947, pp. 421–30.

chapter four

Religion and Human Stress

James Mitchener, in *The Bridges of Toki-ri*, has brought home to us anew the tragedy of sudden "senseless" death. His hero, Brubacher—a jet pilot in the Marine airforce who perished in Korea, a man who had everything to live for—knowingly risked almost certain death to bomb strategic enemy bridges, even though his commanding officer had given him the chance of refusing the mission. Since this was his second tour of combat duty, Brubacher had already done more than his part to defend his society. His wife, who eagerly awaited his return, had also borne her full share of the sacrifices demanded of women in wartime, and therefore had a right to expect some consideration both from her society and perhaps from fate, in return. Yet her plans and hopes were cruelly frustrated, as are those of so many wives, mothers, and sweethearts throughout the world today.

Brubacher's wife knew how her husband had died. More than most wives, because she had visited her husband at sea and had talked with his commanding officer, she understood intellectually the conditions and hazards of jet-plane warfare. She knew, too, that her husband was a brave man who had done his duty; and she also approved intellectually of the United Nations cause for which he had laid down his life. And yet, like all human beings, she was a feeling as well as a thinking creature, and to adjust to her bereavement she needed something more than "this cold knowledge."[1] Mitchener does not tell us what this woman did to bear her grief. Whether she took comfort in memories of her husband, or in her children, or in the understanding of her friends, or in the ritualistic expression of sorrow, or in the religious belief that God had both herself and her husband in His keeping and that somehow He would make all things right in the end, we do not know. We do know, however, that in order to come to terms with her sorrow she would need not only factual knowledge but an interpretation of the tragedy that she could accept emotionally as well. Then only could she go on her way, a whole person, to fulfil her part as mother and citizen in the on-going stream of social life.

The Role of Religion in Stress Situations

In all human societies there are stretches of time when things run smoothly, when social obligations are normally fulfilled, and when men and women play their social roles reasonably secure that their fellows will reciprocate. Men know that they can depend on one another, and in the natural as well as in the social world they know in large measure what they can count on.[2] Hence people are able to plan and can look forward to their plans' fruition. Thus plans made by parents for the rearing and education of their children, marriages and homes are contemplated, fields and vineyards are tended and har-

28

vests anticipated, business and professional activities are marked by planning—all these plans are made with a reasonable hope of their fulfilment. In short, there is a tremendous investment of time and energy, both physical and emotional, of human beings everywhere in the furtherance of such plans, and without this investment of directed energy human societies could hardly be maintained as going concerns.

But though there are periods in most societies when people go about their business without particular strain and the means available to them are adequate to attain the goals for which they have been taught to strive, this is by no means always the case. For there are also crucial situations of stress in the life of all societies when the means available to their members are insufficient to enable them to attain their most cherished goals. Indeed, if human social affairs moved along without uncontrollable and unpredictable accidents and strains, the role of religion in human society, if any, would be a very different matter. Without unanticipated events beyond our control we would be much more likely, as Talcott Parsons has said, to think of the problems of life as mainly practical ones, to be solved by good "horse sense."³ If this situation existed, moreover, then the development and application of scientific techniques might in fact be expected to produce a utopian world.

We know, however, that tragedy and stress inhere in the very nature of the human situation. There is always a gap, of greater or lesser extent, in all societies between the culturally grooved hopes and expectations of men and their fulfilment. Hence practical scientific techniques, however highly developed, can never be adequate to meet all human situations. Men everywhere must adjust to events that they cannot adequately foresee or control. These adjustments may at times be practical, but they are always emotional. In modern industrial societies, to be sure, scientific techniques are available to relieve many stress situations that cannot be met in this way in other types of society; but emotional frustrations remain. Furthermore, in modern industrial societies the extensive development of scientific and technical knowledge has helped to create, indirectly, a number of additional unpredictable and uncontrollable situations. Modern scientific warfare, for example, has possibly added as many frustrations as modern medicine has allayed.

Religion, then, can be thought of from one point of view—though this is by no means the whole picture—as one of the most important means used by man to adjust to situations of stress. Stress situations fall into two main categories.⁴ Both types concern involvements in which human beings have a great emotional investment in a successful outcome. In both cases the outcome is not entirely within human control. The first category includes situations in which individuals or groups are faced by the loss of other human beings who are important to them. The loss may be final, as in the case of death, or it may be a more conditional loss occasioned by the failure of associates to fulfil expected mutual obligations. Children, for instance, who are the objects of so many hopes, may "repay" their parents with indifference or hostility, betrothals and marriage vows may be broken, business and financial obligations may be dishonored, friendships and national loyalties may be betrayed.

In all of these situations emotional as well as practical frustrations are involved. And since, to quote Talcott Parsons once more, human beings cannot just "take it,"⁵ means must be found to adjust both the emotional and the practical aspects of the situation. The example of premature death, with which

we began this chapter, is perhaps the classical type situation in this first category. In a second important category, however, fall those situations in which
largely uncontrollable and unpredictable natural forces may imperil the vital
social concerns of food supply and health. The control of agriculture and the
incidence of disease have been important focal points for religious behavior in
all societies.

Religion as a Mode of Adjustment: The Case of Death

We deliberately chose an example of premature death to illustrate the part
played by religion as a means of adjusting to frustrations in human relationships because of both the universality of this phenomenon and the extreme
frustration and stress it commonly occasions to those who are bereaved.

Death is both unpredictable and ultimately beyond human control. For
though we all know that we will have to die, almost no man knows when death
will occur. "Lord, let me know mine end and the number of my days that I
may be certified how long I have to live," said the Hebrew psalmist, and
thereby gave voice to the most universal of all human uncertainties. No man,
save perhaps the suicide, can plan for his death, much less control it. In part
because of this uncertainty we find religious interpretations of death in every
society. Though religious orientations to death contain many shadings of
belief about life after death, the fundamental feature of these beliefs for social
science is not, as they may be interpreted by some, that they are evidences of
mere so-called wishful thinking. Whatever may be considered the "ultimate"
truth about such matters, sociologically viewed, religious beliefs provide a set
of "mechanisms" by means of which those about to die and those bereaved are
enabled to adjust themselves to the stressful reality.[6]

One sociologist has surmised that in a society in which premature death,
through the application of scientific medicine and the elimination of wars and
accidents, had been abolished so that everyone could count on living out their
threescore years and ten, the part now played by religion in human affairs
might be substantially altered. There is, of course, no immediate prospect of
such a society.* But even in this hypothetical case, so great is the emotional
investment of each individual in his own life that whenever death comes it
must always, in a sense, be premature. Many of us know individuals who at the
age of ninety are full of plans and eager for more life in which their plans may
be realized.

Since the frustration of death is unescapable, human beings have always
oriented themselves to death by means of both religious belief and ritual.
Beliefs about death and afterlife cannot nullify death, of course, but they can
help people to face it, and to serve their societies the better while doing so. To
men like Brubacher, the combat pilot, and indeed to all those to whom the
imminence of death is an apparent probability, the need served by such beliefs

---

* Whether or not we should actually delight in such a scientifically controlled and, so to
say, machine-made, world is of course quite another matter. Fictional attempts to portray
such a world, as, for instance, Aldous Huxley's well-known *Brave New World* seem to suggest that many of the values of human personality that we deem most precious would be
doomed to extinction therein. Perhaps the historian Arnold Toynbee had something of the
same idea in mind when he claimed that the full potential of the spirit of man can only
be evoked as a response to the challenge of the uncontrollable and unpredictable events in
human society and sometimes this very response has made it possible for man to assume a
greater measure of control over his human destiny.

is perhaps more urgent than it is for the majority of more sheltered folk. It need surprise no one that wars create many so-called foxhole religionists.

But even more important for human society are what we have earlier termed the *latent functions* of religious beliefs about death and the dead. For these beliefs define for the living the place of the dead in both the suprasocial and the social scheme of things. These definitions not only serve to reassure the living,* who may be apprehensive in regard to their relationship to the dead or the intentions of the dead towards themselves, but these definitions also have practical social implications.

For example, the anthropologist Reo Fortune tells us that among the Manus people, who live in the Bismarck Archipelago, the spirits of those who have just died are believed to be actively present in the villages of the living, where they function as a kind of moral policemen, custodians of the village mores. In this capacity the ever-watchful spirits of the recently dead are concerned that the financial obligations, as well as the sexual prohibitions, both of which are central to the Manus' system of social values, are strictly observed.[7] Again, the belief of the Chinese that their dead ancestors continue to exist as sacred beings who thrive on the care and respect rendered to them by a long line of descendants, has helped to maintain vital elements in the fabric of their society, namely a veneration for all elders and the strength and cohesion of the greater family, so that Chinese society for thousands of years has been notable for its conservatism and stability. In contrast, the creeds of some Christian churches teach that the dead are ever living and spiritually active members of a "communion of saints" that includes all Christian souls, both "dead" and living. This latter belief, especially in medieval times, constituted a dynamic psychic resource on which a developing society could draw.

We may point out in passing that the repercussions of religious beliefs concerning the dead on the social life of the living should make it clear that religious belief in general is something different from the acceptance of a set of philosophical ideas. The later may have no implications for human conduct, but a belief is not *religious*, as Durkheim understood it, unless it is taken seriously, that is, unless something is done about it, either directly or indirectly.

Equally significant for the society is the *ritualization* of death. Whatever meaning death may have for the person most immediately concerned, for those who are bereaved it inevitably entails the severance of a whole network of social relationships and mutual obligations. Though the following statement may perhaps appear to some as callous, and for the religionist it represents only a small part of what he regards as the truth, from the this-worldly point of view of the sociologist the main social functions performed by the religionizing of death are the rehabilitation of the bereaved and the repairing of the broken web of social relationships. For a wider social community, as well as those immediately bereaved, is affected by the passing of an individual, especially an individual holding a responsible position. Therefore the society's temporary breach in its system of mutual obligations must be closed and its normal ways of life continued.

Religious ritual in relation to death, then, serves to reaffirm the social solidarity of the larger social group and to place the latter's support at the disposal

---

* It may be argued that the beliefs of some religions about the role of the dead are terrifying rather than reassuring. But even if this is granted, there is at least some reassurance in having the area of terror defined and delimited.

of the bereaved. This function of religious ritual has been observed in ancient and modern, primitive and civilized societies. And though the forms of many of these rituals may perhaps seem strange—and at times even laughable—to us, this does not mean that they are mere "errors," soon to be outmoded by the advancement of science. Though the forms are likely to be modified, these rituals, if they are to satisfy human needs, can never be based solely on science or common sense.

In fact, some of the older forms of ritual no doubt fulfilled this social function more effectively than certain of our more modern forms. However, in contemporary urban societies the nature of orientations towards death and emotional needs concerning bereavement have also undergone considerable change, inevitably leading to modifications of rituals. Many individuals today feel uncomfortable in the presence of older forms of ritual.* Though members of modern communities, especially in rural areas, still attend funerals in order to demonstrate their standing in and solidarity with local groups as well as to give support to the bereaved, the wakes and wailing ceremonies of earlier peasant societies most clearly reveal this rallying around the survivors.

These wailings and wakes at one time served a more personal function for the bereaved, a function that is now more likely to be performed by individual friends, understanding ministers, or even by psychiatrists. For many of the earlier rites had a quasi-psychiatric function. Though the fact is difficult to face, considerable ambivalence exists in our emotions concerning the dead. Survivors may resent former actions of the deceased or may feel guilty about their own acts of commission or omission with respect to the dead. Either situation is likely to induce some psychic conflict, conflict which may hamper the social participation of the bereaved. Some of the more "primitive" rituals dramatized this internal conflict, and so served to "drain off" ambivalent emotions and thus acted as a catharsis for feelings of guilt as well as grief. The funeral rites of the Australian Warramunga, for example, in which the participants dramatized self-punitive feelings by acting out extremes of self-mutilation, were in all probability an effective means of allaying self-crippling guilt, even though this method is certainly not one which we today would care to emulate.[8]

Lugubrious as they may be, however, death rituals almost always culminate in a positive, affirmative note. For death, like birth, is an integral part of the on-going life process, a total process to which we all ultimately contribute. Without death, the eliminator, there could be no continuing life. But even when this positive affirmation is obscure, in many societies the termination of the death rituals, which furnish occasion for the gathering of a group of otherwise scattered individuals, is marked by discreet feasting and circumspect conviviality. Each society has its particular traditions, to be sure, but there are counterparts in many places of the Yorkshireman who said to his friend as he partook of the succulent ham sandwiches customary at funeral "teas," "Eh, lad, Ah've not 'ad such a good time, no, not since my wife's sister was buried!" Though those immediately bereaved are hardly likely to enter fully into this

---

* One of the results of the juxtaposition in our modern world of societies of different types (which we discussed in Chapter Two) is that individuals accustomed to living in one type of society are, at the time of their bereavement, subjected, even against their will, to death rituals customary in a society of a different type. This fact not infrequently is an occasion of acute distress for such individuals.

aspect of the occasion, yet their obligation, frequently affirmed by the culture, to provide food and drink for the assembled gathering is a symbolical means by which they affirm even in their grief that the living too must be considered and that in spite of death life must go on.

We have chosen to discuss at some length these beliefs and rituals surrounding death as an illuminating example of the social and psychological functions performed by religion in the type of situation that we place in our first category: strains and tensions pertaining to upsetting aspects of social relationships. The reader is invited to explore for himself further the part played by religion in other stress situations of this order.

Religion as a Mode of Adjustment: Unpredictable Natural Forces

In our second category fall situations in which unpredictable and uncontrollable natural forces place human survival in jeopardy. Food is essential to life and health, and the fear of famine is often deep seated. The success of the harvest is a vital concern all over the earth. The exposure of agricultural products to the uncertainty of weather guarantees an area of precariousness in which human intelligence and skill may fail to obtain the results on which life depends. This area of precariousness is most evident in those cultures in which empirical techniques are least developed and weather conditions are most violent and least predictable, but it is never entirely absent. For man has never been able to control entirely the outcome of this concern of such crucial importance to him.

The Pueblo Indians of the American Southwest, for example, are skilful in preparing land and planting and cultivating corn, yet harvests are sometimes lacking because rainfall is beyond their control. Similarly in the West Indies today, where the prosperity of certain areas is almost entirely dependent on the success of the banana crop, a devastating hurricane can destroy the crop at the very time it is coming to fruition. Even in regions where technical skill is highly developed some uncertainty remains—grasshoppers may batten on Nebraska wheat or a late frost may decimate the Georgia peach crop.

Agriculture is an important stress situation in which what anthropologists have termed *magic* is a frequently employed means of adjustment. Shortly the precise meaning of magic and its distinction from religion will be discussed. Here we should note that though the ends of magic and religion are not the same, both involve techniques of adjustment to strains brought about by uncertainty. Hence magic, in this context, may be thought of as continuous with religion; in fact, in most agricultural societies magic and religion are closely intertwined. In such societies the rhythm of the seasons and their attendant agricultural activities are characterized by a round of magicoreligious observances. Dances and incantations mark the spring planting, and by means of fertility dances and sacrifices the favor of the rain gods is sought or the gods of the swollen rivers propitiated. Harvest, as we know, is an occasion for ritual thanksgiving.

Of what use to the society are these magicoreligious practices? No man can make crops grow by magic or religion alone. Nor does it seem to be true that so-called primitive peoples possess such limited mentalities—as the French anthropologist Levy-Bruhl professed to believe—that they are unaware of the essential difference between the effects of magicoreligious techniques and practical agricultural procedures.* The anthropologist Malinowski, whose studies of the Trobriand islanders were cited earlier, illuminated the function of religious-magic by showing that the Trobrianders, at any rate, were well aware of this difference. These natives have great respect for such technical know-how as they do possess, but they are also aware of its limitations. The magicoreligious practices which accompany their agriculture and fishing are supplements, not substitutes, for their practical techniques. They do not believe that they can make up for their failure to cultivate their gardens efficiently by the use of more and better magic.⁹ What then is the function of their religious-magic?

Malinowski contended that the reinforcement of self-confidence in the face of situations of strain is the most important function performed by religious-magic. Dances, incantations, and spells help people to adjust to strains by providing opportunities to dramatize their psychological anxieties. Religious-magic invokes a sense of "doing something about it" in undertakings of uncertainty in which practical techniques alone cannot guarantee success. On the basis of his Trobriand researches Malinowski came to the conclusion that when great uncertainty about the outcome is associated with activities vital to human societies, the use of magicoreligious or other comparable techniques as means for allaying tension and promoting adjustment is inevitable.¹⁰

This generalization, however, does not imply that magicoreligious techniques invariably have positive social functions. One of the negative consequences of magicoreligious practices is the fact that once such means are adopted there develops a vested interest in their continuance, often blocking the acceptance of more efficient techniques even when they are available. This is a common problem in many "backward" regions of the world today.

Physical and psychic health is another area in which magicoreligious methods are commonly employed, ranging from the spiritual healing authorized by some Christian churches to the practices of witch doctors. Among the Navaho Indians, for example, the main focus of religious behavior is in the area of health and disease. Among the Christian Scientists also health in all its aspects is a chief concern of religious activity. Here again religion and magic aid social survival in so far as they "act as a tonic" and help those concerned to tap psychic resources from which they might otherwise be cut off. Yet their use may also hamper a society's well-being if the adoption of scientific methods of tried effectiveness is blocked.

Religion and Magic as Alternative Means of Adjustment

From our discussion so far it should be clear that religion supplies an important method, though not the only one, by which man meets situations of stress. Other important means employed are magic and science. We pointed out earlier in this chapter that, as methods of adjustment, magic may be thought of continuous with religion and that in concrete institutional life magic and religion frequently coexist as a blend. We must differentiate between the two. The means employed by both magic and religion are alike in being nonempirical, but they differ significantly in the ends they seek. Reli-

---

* In this respect they are of one mind with the old Vermont farmer of many a pulpit story. When the minister visited him after church and congratulated him on what the "Lord had wrought" on his recently cleared half acre, the farmer replied laconically, "Yes, but you should have seen it when the Lord had it all to Himself!"

gion's goals are oriented to the nonempirical, the other-worldly, the supernatural. Though religion is often concerned with the physical and social welfare of human beings, it always has a transcendental point of reference. This is not true of magic. The ends the practitioner of magic seeks are in the everyday human world.

Furthermore, the religious worshipper, as distinct from the magician or his clients, is constrained by an attitude of awe and reverence toward the sacred ends which he pursues. For him the ends must inhere in the means. The user of magic, on the other hand, is "in business" for practical and arbitrarily chosen results. For him reverence and awe are out of place because he is a manipulator of the supernatural for his own private ends and those of his clients rather than a worshipper of it. To snare a fowl, to net a school of fish, to keep animals from the crops, to heal disease, or to secure the compliance of a lover he may utter his spells almost casually, in a normal everyday voice, as one who beseeches no favor but expects rather an automatic reaction to correct methods. By means of his magical knowledge, which is often very private property, the magician believes that he can control or coerce the supernatural and thereby produce concrete, observable results.

Moreover the content of magic and of religion differ. Religious systems, particularly in their higher developments, may encompass the whole of life; they may provide a total theory of both the supernatural and human society. The content of magic, on the other hand, constitutes no unified inclusive theory but is apt to be atomistic, something like an old-fashioned book of recipes or a home doctor manual.

In practice, as we have seen, magic and religion are often closely intermixed. However, two main varieties of magic may be distinguished. One kind of magic, such as that practiced by the Trobrianders in the cultivation of their coral gardens and in fishing, is used for group purposes and has much in common with religion. Such quasi-religious techniques are sometimes known as white magic. The most secret antisocial varieties of magic, such as witchcraft and obeah, in contrast, have been termed black magic. One way of viewing the distinction between religion and magic is to regard each as occupying a polar extreme on a continuum. From this viewpoint the purest, most other-worldly manifestations of "higher" religions represents one extreme and black magic the other.

But there are many subtle blendings of religious-magical behavior along this hypothetical continuum. In addition, several types of behavior most commonly thought of as religious on examination are seen to fluctuate between the magical and religious poles. At the religious pole, for instance, prayer is exemplified by the belief of Brother Lawrence for whom prayer is identical with the "practice of the presence of God"; whereas prayer at the magical pole is illustrated by the Tibetan's water-driven wheel, a mechanical contrivance that continues its "prayers" even while the worshipper sleeps. Or again, take sacrifice. At the magical extreme, sacrifice may be an attempt to coerce, in a way, the supernatural with gifts; yet sacrifice may be conceived in the meaning of the Hebrew psalmist who came to his God not with a burnt offering but with the sacrifice of a "broken and a contrite heart"—clearly a religious view.

We noted above some of the social functions of white, or religious, magic. Before leaving this topic we should raise the question of the possible contributions of black magic to the maintenance of human societies. Some scholars

36 — Religion and Society

maintain that from a psychological point of view witchcraft, the best-known instance of black magic, may operate to relieve group frustrations and distress by serving to project hostile emotions so frequently associated with stress situations outside the group itself, or, alternatively, to focus these hostile feelings on a limited, special segment of the social group. In other words, black magic may help the group to maintain its internal cohesion and solidarity in the face of social stress.*

This function of magic is clarified in Clyde Kluckhohn's study *Navaho Witchcraft*. Kluckhohn shows how witchcraft in this case is associated with the almost unbearable psychological and social pressures occasioned in part by the extreme isolation of family life in a society of widely scattered sheep raisers. Navaho culture prohibits all manifestations of overt hostility among family members; nevertheless, as psychiatric research conducted by Kluckhohn and others among the Navahos brings out, their living conditions stimulate considerable ambivalence of feeling and hostile (as well as cooperative) emotions. But most Navahos do not dare to give vent to these tabooed sentiments within the family circle itself, suffering guilt and anxiety if they admit even to themselves that they do in fact entertain such feelings. In this dilemma the assumed existence of malevolent witches provides the Navaho people with approved targets for their repressed hate, and by means of this black magic they can "get back at" their enemies, both real and imaginary.[11]

Since the Navaho economy might break down if individual families in their scattered hogans are not able to cooperate effectively in their sheep raising, and since witchcraft provides an agency for the relief of psychic guilt that might otherwise reach unmanageable proportions, in the absence of alternative techniques the latent function of witchcraft may be said to be positive. However, whether among the Navahos or others, any relief from stress which witchcraft may afford is bought at a large social cost, evidenced not only in the possible victimization of the witches themselves, but also in the widespread fear and suspicion that witchcraft keeps alive in a social group. A still further cost of magical practices, as we have already indicated, is that once they have become accepted customs, they act to block the adoption of technically superior means to handle stress situations. In the case of the Navaho tribe, for example, in which witchcraft and black magic are closely linked with the maintenance of health, the acceptance of the aid of modern scientific medicine has been retarded.

Religion and Science as Alternative Modes of Adjustment

Science supplies men with practical empirical means for adjusting to practical empirical situations. Whereas in religion both the ends sought and the means used are nonempirical. Moreover science, in marked contrast to magic, employs practical empirical means, though both science and magic seek practical, empirical ends.*

Science, unlike magic or religion, may at first glance seem to be the very

* Other students may feel that this line of reasoning constitutes a somewhat strained attempt to find a function for magic and may prefer more simply to regard much magic as dysfunctional.

* These distinctions between religion, magic, and science are consistent with those drawn by Malinowski and by Durkheim and have been utilized more recently by Parsons and other writers.

acme of modernity. This is because we are apt to think of science almost solely in its familiar highly developed form. Very simple techniques, however, can be scientific in principle. In fact science is as old as society and, indeed, human culture could not have developed without some minimal scientific techniques. Long before the arrival of Europeans, for example, the American Indians of the Southwest had developed methods of cultivating corn which were and still are of demonstrable effectiveness in crop production. The fact that they did not achieve the results made possible by a more developed technology does not negate the scientific character of the simpler methods.

The conspicuous achievements of modern science and its consequent prestige convince many people today that science is the dominant method used by man to achieve his many purposes and to adjust to stresses of various kinds. Science's record of success in these respects is clearly impressive; there can be no doubt that it performs from many points of view positive social functions.[12] The question remains, however, whether or not the functions of science are unconditionally positive; for science does not apply itself but is applied by social beings to social purposes in terms of social values. Hence it may be asked if science, like religion and magic, does not also at times create additional stresses while alleviating others. A related question and one more intimately connected with our central theme, namely, the social function of religion in stress situations, also arises: Does religion as a means of adjustment to stress situations become less important in human affairs as scientific means become more effective?

These questions like those raised in the preceding chapter should be discussed in terms of various social contexts or particular types of societies. Therefore we shall use once more our threefold typology of societies in order to suggest possible answers.

Magic, Science, and Religion in Different Types of Societies

In societies of *type one*, of which the Trobriand Islands furnish one example, magicoreligious methods of adjustment are apt to be fairly dominant and science and technology are relatively little developed and used. In nonliterate societies religion is frequently inextricably blended with magic, and magicoreligious means are utilized in adjusting to a number of stress situations which are often handled religiously in societies of type two or scientifically in societies of type three.

The magicoreligious blend in these societies, however, is by no means of a uniform nature. In one society, for example, the main area of anxiety and stress may be concerned with assuring prowess in warfare, in another, with the hazards of agriculture, and elsewhere with the threats to the maintenance of physical health.[13] In each case the magicoreligious means are focused upon an area of special anxiety and stress which is important in the experience of the society in question. Frequently though not invariably, situations of stress in societies of type one are closely related to uncertainties concerning the basic conditions for assuring physical survival.

In societies of *type two* scientific technology is more developed than in societies of type one and therefore science furnishes a somewhat more effective means of providing for physical needs. Scientific theory, however, is not highly developed, especially in comparison with societies of type three.

Magic, both white and black, still functions overtly and covertly in these societies. Much popular religious magic survives from an earlier day, witchcraft is endemic, and the hysteria of witchhunting recurs periodically in times of special stress—as the history of the European Middle Ages illustrates.

Religion in the type two society typically attempts to free itself from entanglement with magic and to become differentiated into a fairly self-consistent ethical system. The great founders of the ethical religions of the world aided this development, their teachings showing all of them to have emphatically repudiated magical methods. In spite of these teachings, however, magic remains in societies of this type as an important means of adjustment to stress situations for a great number of people. While the official religious organizations often disavow magic, they are forced to make compromises with it and a great deal of earlier magic is rebaptized in the name of religion.

Though important areas of stress in these societies still remain in connection with securing the fundamentals for sheer physical survival, their increasing complexity gives rise to additional strains of a social and psychological nature. The mere acceptance of custom is no longer quite enough. Men are beginning to demand ethical reasons for the inequalities of institutional arrangements and, often, for the condition of man himself. These psychological and social strains are characteristically dealt with by distinctively religious means. Religion often helps in the adjustment to the psychic tensions occasioned by the uncertainty men feel about their origin and destiny and it furnishes in these societies the most commonly accepted official cosmologies. In addition, religion reassures people about the rightness of the basic institutions of organized social life, thus supporting family relationships and the reciprocal obligations of government and the economic order.

Societies of type three feature a highly dynamic science, both theoretical and applied, which is increasingly used as a practical means of adjusting to stress situations of many kinds. Science supersedes magical and religious methods in meeting problems of physical health and of maintaining a steady supply of food.

The use of magic, however, is not entirely obsolete in these scientifically oriented societies, though it is applied to rather different types of stress situations than in societies of types one and two. So-called old-fashioned magic as a means of adjustment to personal hazards still persists in the form of semi-archaic survivals; beliefs, such as in the gardener's green thumb, and practices like the avoidance of walking under ladders, are retained by some individuals half in jest and half in earnest.* Moreover organized religions, in greater or lesser degree, tend to discard or reinterpret the older form of religious magic.

These secular societies, on the other hand, develop characteristic kinds of stress situations, less associated with the precariousness of natural forces than with the hazards of economic arrangements and job security. A new streamlined secularized magic is used for the coercion of the secular deities: the gods of money, success, and power. The weekly sale of millions of astrology and numerology magazines, for example, testify to the thriving character of this type of magic. Wherever money, success, and power are most assiduously cultivated soothsayers of all kinds batten on rich and poor alike. Big-time gamblers in the financial districts, small-time gamblers in numbers and cards, many

---

* Students will recognize various examples of semimagic practiced by themselves or by their fellows, for example, love magic and examination magic.

aspirants to stardom in athletics, stage, or screen, or even in politics are among those who seek their aid.

In addition, the increasing use of science and its products helps to create new stress situations that magic is sometimes called upon to alleviate. Modern science as applied to warfare and transportation has exposed the members of these societies to frightening new physical dangers. The use of magic by many individuals who face extreme hazards, such as air pilots and combat troops, not only persists but also continues to exist side by side with the most modern technical equipment and gadgetry. The controller of a supersonic dashboard may treasure in the depths of his pocket an ancient rabbit's foot.[14]

Again, the modern city, itself in large part a product of science, is marked by social and psychic loneliness and rootlessness of many individuals, some of whom are recruited by the new magical-religious cults that flourish in metropolitan areas (as well as in deprived and disturbed sections of the rural population).

What then is the role of religion in the adjustment to both the older and newer types of stress situations in societies of type three? The older types have not been eliminated, though they have been mitigated, by the application of science. Nature's threats to human survival—floods, tornadoes, uncontrollable disease—are more likely to be viewed as occasional acts of God than as ever-present hazards to survival. The basic requirements of health and food supply are largely assured by modern technology. Nevertheless—and in spite of the fact that even rainfall is sometimes artificially produced by "seeding the clouds"*—adjustment to sporadic natural calamities is aided by religious as well as scientific techniques.

The psychic tensions engendered by the great unanswerable questions "Whence does man come?, Why is he here?, and Whither is he going?," persist. And the answers to these questions are partly intellectual and partly emotional in nature. The intellectual component commonly includes an explanation of the physical nature of man and his place in the universe as embodied for example, in modern cosmologies. In societies of type two religion supplies the officially accepted cosmologies, but in modern secular societies science provides the most commonly used explanations, and earlier religious cosmology is continually reevaluated in the light of the growing accumulation of scientific findings. Modern science, however, leaves unanswered the basic moral and emotional questions about human destiny. Present-day psychology and psychiatry possibly help to allay some of the anxiety and stress created by these fundamental uncertainties. In addition, prolongation of the human life span and general increase in health and comfort enable many individuals to postpone facing these potentially disturbing issues. But sooner or later in most lives these questions must be faced. At that point religious faith and philosophy continue to supply an important means of human adjustment.

Finally, the new stress situations engendered by scientific technology itself pose new problems for religion. The use of the hydrogen bomb and jet planes in modern warfare has confronted all mankind, especially city dwellers, with the threat of mass destruction. Furthermore, a highly complex mode of living,

---

* During a recent drought in New York, when the municipal government employed an expert to seed the clouds, the following cartoon appeared in *The New Yorker*: Inside a church through whose Gothic windows the rain could be seen falling in torrents, two cassocked clerics looking dubiously at this scene asked of each other "Is it *his* or ours?"

featured by close functional interdependence but also by impersonality, has introduced unprecedented social and psychological pressures. These pressures emphasize the need in societies of type three for the development of religious as well as scientific means for dealing with new types of stress. But the growth of new religious interpretations and applications is markedly less dynamic than the development of science. This differential is partly the result of the great prestige that has been achieved by science and scientific activity in modern society.

The members of modern society, we believe, manifest a dual trend regarding the use of religion as a means of adjustment to stress. Many individuals have almost entirely discarded the personal use of religion. Others, especially in times of personal or society-wide distress, are reaffirming religion. Apparently a large number of people alternate between these two patterns, both of which require more careful sociological study than they have received.

The assimilation and reinterpretation of evolving human knowledge has marked religious thought throughout human history. It is not surprising, therefore, that in societies of type three religious leaders are attempting to assimilate new scientific knowledge, particularly psychiatry. They see this as an essential task if religion is to be a more effective means for coping with the stress situations of the modern world.

Footnotes to Chapter Four

1. Davis, Kingsley: *Human Society*, New York, The Macmillan Company, 1949, p. 517.
2. Cf. Parsons, Talcott: *Religious Perspectives of College Teaching in Sociology and Social Psychology*, New Haven, Edward W. Hazen Foundation, 1951, p. 10.
3. *Ibid.*, p. 10.
4. *Ibid.*, p. 11–2.
5. *Ibid.*, p. 13.
6. *Ibid.*, p. 11.
7. Fortune, Reo: *Manus Religion*, Philadelphia, The American Philosophical Society, 1935, pp. 49–50.
8. Durkheim, Émile: *The Elementary Forms of the Religious Life.* Translated by E. W. Swain. Glencoe, Ill., The Free Press, 1947, pp. 390–403.
9. Malinowski, Bronislaw: *Magic, Science and Religion*, Glencoe, Ill., The Free Press, 1948, pp. 12–3.
10. *Ibid.*, pp. 67–70.
11. Kluckhohn, Clyde: *Navaho Witchcraft*, Cambridge, Mass., Peabody Museum, 1944, pp. 54–5.
12. Cf. Barber, Bernard: *Science and the Social Order*, Glencoe, Ill., The Free Press, 1952, pp. 5–6 and Chapter Three.
13. Benedict, Ruth: Chapter 14 in Franz Boas, et al.: *General Anthropology*, Boston, D. C. Heath & Company, 1938, pp. 633–4.
14. Davis, Kingsley: *op. cit.*, p. 541.

chapter five

Religion, the Problem of Meaning, and Society

The Problem of Meaning in Individual and Social Experience

In the preceding chapter we discussed some of the means which religion makes available to societies and their members to help them to adjust to the uncertainties and strains of life. In the present chapter we propose to consider the role of religion in providing a framework of meaning within which human beings interpret in moral terms their personal distresses and successes as well as the past history and present circumstances of their societies. In other words, we are moving from the analysis of religion's contribution in answering some of the crucial *hows* of social life to a consideration of its related function in dealing with some of the equally crucial *whys*. In more formal language, we are passing from a consideration of the *conative* aspects of religion's social role to a discussion of its *cognitive* aspects.

Throughout the ages religion has given man not only rituals that provide emotional relief and techniques that fortify faith and thus enable him to carry on, but also generalized intellectual interpretations that have helped him to make moral sense out of his total life experience. Religion has aided people in answering the question of why untoward things happen. Some answer to this question—which may be asked and answered on very different levels—is no doubt a necessity for human beings if they are to accept and assimilate their frustrations. The ability to find meaning in seemingly needless suffering, for example, is an essential condition for suffering to be used by the individual for the good of the group.

The Biblical character of Job epitomizes this eternal human why. For Job, by discharging both his social and religious obligations, had striven to revere the sacred values that were exemplified in the divine commandments as he knew them. What kind of Being, then, must God be to let him suffer so much? When Job turned from the contemplation of his own miserable lot to think of the fate of his fellow men, he was forced to the conclusion that most human beings were sunk in misery and injustice. Thus he was led to ask God for an explanation not only of his own wretchedness but of that of all mankind. Job confronted what is often referred to as *the problem of evil*.

Job was puzzled and distressed too by the apparent injustice with which a supposedly righteous God distributed His rewards and punishments in human society.[1] If God was righteous, why did He cause the righteous man Job to be stricken while on every side the "ungodly flourished like the green bay tree?" Why does not God guarantee that people get their just deserts? In the same vein the flyer's widow in Michener's story might well have asked, "Why should a just God allow her husband to perish when many younger men with

41

less combat service are holding down safe and profitable desk jobs at home?"

These disparities in men's fortunes and misfortunes are not readily explainable in accordance with ordinary human standards of what is fair and right. Therefore an important function of religion is to "justify the ways of God to man." Put otherwise, religion has the function of assigning moral meaning to human experiences, which might seem otherwise a "tale told by an idiot, full of sound and fury, signifying nothing."

We have stated the problem of meaning in an individual context for the sake of both poignancy and clarity. This problem, however, is not essentially different when we consider it in the context of entire societies, each with its particular set of interacting institutions. Each human society may be viewed, as it were, from the *outside* and as differentiated from other human societies; but each society also may be studied as a social system from the *inside*. When we look at societies from the outside, that is, in historical perspective and in relation to other societies, we may ask why some tribes and nations attain power and success while others seemed destined to poverty and impotence. When we view societies from the inside, we are confronted with inequalities in the distribution of wealth, power, and happiness among the members, inequities that inevitably stimulate moral interpretations of the social order.

The Problem of the Meaning of Society Itself

Every society that has persisted for any appreciable length of time amidst the wars and rivalries that have generally accompanied group life has developed some moral interpretation of its own way of life—some explanation of the problem of *societal meaning*. For if the members of a society are to fulfil their social obligations, there must be available a morally acceptable explanation of the society's particular system of institutional arrangements, including its social disparities.

Undoubtedly a larger measure of equality and human justice marks the social arrangements of some societies than others, yet in no society does the actual distribution of its social rewards and punishments conform entirely to ideal requirements of justice—insofar as human beings in a particular society agree as to what they mean by that term. Hence in all societies contrasts between ideal and practice require explanation and interpretation.[2] Equally important is the fact that to date no human group has been able to evolve an explanation of the meaning of its social system that is morally watertight, without drawing upon at least some elements outside the realm of empirical common sense. Apart from the acceptance of the viewpoint which regards human injustice as brute fact and social life as morally meaningless, no empirical or common-sense answer is readily available to the questions posed by the inequalities and inequities of social systems.

The above considerations provide the general context for the role that religion (which by definition embraces the nonempirical in its purview) plays in making moral interpretations of human history and social arrangements. For all attempted moral solutions in purely empirical terms tend to break down in the face of glaring adverse balances on the moral side of the social ledger. Hence explanations of societal meaning which have gained wide acceptance invariably, in order to balance the moral books, introduce nonempirical or even completely supernatural elements. A common example of the use of such nonempirical balancing factors are the religious beliefs in the existence of future lives in worlds in which the unmerited sufferings of those who have died receive supernatural redress and evil-doers their just deserts.

At times this moral balancing is thought of as occurring in the future of *this* world. The travail of an entire nation or tribe or social class may be tolerable to the group concerned because of a deeply-held belief in a promised land of freedom, equity, and justice in the historical future.[3] On closer examination most beliefs of this kind may also be shown to be nonempirical in nature, particularly when the earthly utopia is not immediately attained. As the realization of the promised land fades into the indefinite future the original concrete goal takes on nonempirical overtones. What was at first a goal to be worked for changes to a treasured dream for future generations. Finally this dream may become an article of faith whereby present sufferings may be more patiently endured. Thus the wheel has swung full circle, and the originally empirical goal has become a sacred value.

Our discussion of religious interpretations then will first treat briefly societies in their entirety and consider variant ways in which their history has been given meaning by religion. We shall then view in more detail the problem of societal meaning as it affects the interrelations of various groups and institutions within societies. Special consideration will be given those groups and institutions of principal significance in defining differential social positions and in allocating rewards and punishments.

One of our main interests is the meaning ascribed by certain religions to the differences in position and prestige of various social classes. In other words, we shall consider some of the religious interpretations of systems of social stratification. Differences in class standing are closely correlated with the distribution of economic wealth and political power. Therefore we shall also discuss religious interpretations of the meaning of economic and political institutions, and especially religious explanations of the use and acquisition of material wealth and the exercise and abuse of political authority.

What Determines Religious Interpretations?

In the religious interpretations of the meaning of social arrangements presented below the reader will not fail to observe a high degree of consistency between the religious doctrine and actual institutional arrangements. To what degree a particular religion has impressed its own ethical meaning on a given society's thoughtways or, conversely, to what extent religious doctrine merely reflects or rationalizes the political and economic status quo, has been and remains to some degree a central question for scholars in this field. We do not, however, propose to concern ourselves with this problem at this point.

However, a word of sociological caution is in order. Some readers may perhaps hold the opinion congenial to Marxist thought that all religious interpretations are merely rationalizations, possibly even deliberate and hypocritical ones, which meet the interests of dominant classes.

In reply to this point of view it must be stressed that all idea-systems which have been accepted by an entire society or by large segments of a social order are the products of many years of interacting influences. Such influences include groups concerned with the promulgation and maintenance of religious and ethical values, as well as economic and political groups, including of course dominant power groups. Though particular moral interpretations of the social order often are highly satisfactory to these dominant groups, the extent to which they are deliberate inventions of the latter can easily be exaggerated. On the other hand we must also point out that no religious ethic, even in its purest and most "original" form, was ever developed in complete isolation from the currents of opinion about social, economic, and political conditions. This statement holds for all the great religious systems, whether formulated first by Moses, Buddha, Mohammed, Christ, or Calvin.

Consequently the following discussion makes no attempt to establish the independence or priority of material and economic factors on the one hand and religious and spiritual factors on the other. Rather we present some of the situations, both historical and contemporary, in which explanations of the meaning of the social world have been couched in religious terms and reinforced with religious values. We shall also indicate how these solutions are generally consistent with political, economic, and other social institutions of the societies in question.

Religious Interpretations of the Social Order

Adversity and Religious Beliefs

The classic example of a religious explanation of the meaning of the suffering of an entire society is the doctrine evolved by the Jewish people. At the height of their religious creativity the Jews worked out, though gradually, a moral interpretation of the meaning of their society that was of a more universal, comprehensive, and revolutionary nature than had previously been developed by any other group. In the earlier phases of their history their existence as a people was given meaning by their having been chosen as the faithful servants of a single sacred being, Jehovah, who had revealed His Will to them in the Commandments through Moses. In the light of this faith they took possession, under Joshua, of the promised land of Canaan. Their moral interpreters, the prophets, explained many of their later calamities as being the result of their failure to fulfil Jehovah's Commandments. During their captivity by the Babylonians and Persians it must have seemed to these people that their service to Jehovah, imperfect as it was, was at least more worthy than that of the heathen around them and hence their long-continued sufferings must have appeared as both cruel and undeserved.

In these times of bitter adversity the earlier, more limited religious interpretation of their history and experience gradually broke down. Why should they endure prolonged travail when the kingdoms of the heathen, who neither knew Jehovah nor worshipped Him, flourished mightily? By asking this very question, however, they had been driven to think of Jehovah as the God of the surrounding nations as well as of their own people.

The mental anguish entailed in the attempt to wrest a moral meaning from such tremendous apparent injustice has been recorded by Hebrew psalmists and prophets. A later prophet, a nameless genius known as the second Isaiah, likened the destiny of his people to that of Jehovah's "Suffering Servant"; and their tragic burdens then became a central part of the plan of the Creator and Ruler of the Universe for the salvation of all humankind. This was a high and terrible destiny indeed, but this doctrine enabled the prophet to present a moral and meaningful interpretation of the history of his people.

The keystone of this interpretation consists of course in a nonempirical belief in the existence of a single supreme supernatural being who is deeply involved in the entire course of human history, including that of the Jewish people. There can be no purely scientific grounds for either accepting or rejecting this interpretation. On the other hand it is a matter of record that this nonscientific doctrine has had tremendous practical consequences for the survival of the Jews. Neither the persecution of pagans and Christians nor dispersal to the ends of the earth, nor, more recently, Russian pogroms and Nazi gas ovens have extinguished the religious and cultural vitality of this people.

A secondary solution of the problem of societal meaning, a solution utilized by the Jews in situations of desperate crisis, is the messianic one.[4] Jewish doctrine in this instance is the prototype of the kind of interpretation which has evolved in a number of small, weak societies faced by the possibility of cultural extinction or otherwise without hope. The belief in the imminent coming of a Messiah, or supernatural deliverer, who by means of other-worldly power will right the wrongs of a particular society and thereby usher in a new era of justice and righteousness, clearly accents supernatural explanation. Messianic doctrine is largely a product of desperation, resorted to when a social group can visualize little possibility of continuance. Various societies if faced with impending cultural extinction by the advance of a dominant group, will resort to messianism as did the Jewish people when threatened by the destruction of the Jerusalem Temple by imperial Rome. For example, messianic cults have grown up among certain dying tribes of American Indians.[5] The British colonial governments have been confronted with messianic revolts, such as that of the Mahdi, among subject peoples. Today we read of new outcroppings of messianic movements in Africa and elsewhere. The fact that such unrealistic beliefs sometimes arouse sufficient vitality in a deprived people to resist effectively a much stronger power, bears striking witness to the vital importance to the society concerned of some acceptable solution in moral terms for the meaning of its existence.

Success and Religious Interpretations: The Case of Imperialism

Both types of religious belief we have just discussed are moral interpretations of societal adversity. Almost equally important for a society is a morally acceptable explanation of its successes. Since a successful society often enjoys its worldly accomplishments at the expense of less fortunate peoples, it is frequently driven to finding a moral formula that will not only provide positive meaning for its own good fortune, but also help to diminish any guilt its members may feel about the less happy situation of other groups.[6] Such explanations may stress the superior worth of the members of the successful group and emphasize as well the benefits conferred by their social dominance. Most great imperialistic societies, including Rome, Britain, Soviet Russia, and even the United States, have developed moral formulas of this sort, marked by at least some nonfactual elements. The introduction of these nonempirical factors is all but inevitable, since the exercise of rulership over subject peoples always involves some degree of exploitation, and neither the benefit conferred by the rule nor the superiority of the rulers is necessarily self-evident to mere common sense. Hence justifications of imperialism solely in factual terms have never entirely stood the test of moral adequacy.

A familiar illustration of a moral formula is the one that was current among the British when they were at the height of their imperial success. To many a Victorian Christian the thought that his country had been chosen by God to shoulder the "white man's burden" and to bring the benefits of British civilization and Christianity to "lesser breeds without the law," made the undoubted fact that his country had subjugated and exploited many people socially legitimate and morally acceptable. Though a few hard-boiled rationalists among nineteenth-century Britishers were capable of accepting matter-of-fact explanations of their country's success as implied in the caustic couplet

> Whatever happens we have got
> The maxim gun which they have not

most members of Victorian society would not have slept comfortably had they been required to believe that Britain's imperial rule was justified by sheer force alone. Moreover, such a nonmoral interpretation probably would not have induced a sufficient number of Britons to persevere with the practical and sometimes uncomfortable and lonely tasks necessary to maintain the empire. Some interpretation of the meaning of imperial success acceptable in terms of current morality, such as we have described and which Kipling's famous poem *Recessional* epitomizes, was needed both for the psychic comfort of British society and the mobilization of the vitality of the empire builders.*

An inseparable part of this interpretation was a belief in the superiority of the white man, another nonempirical element in the moral formula. For the most part this belief was an unthinking assumption, common to many peoples with respect to their own group. When this assumption was challenged, many British (and Americans) were inclined to justify it on biblical, and therefore highly moral, grounds. The Book of Genesis was cited as authority for the belief that God created different races of men[7] and that in the wisdom of the Creator, these races were created of unequal worth. Various scholars have pointed out that prevalent ideas of racial superiority came into prominence when, after the seventeenth century, European whites began to expand their rule over many colored peoples. Nonscientific theories of qualitative differences between races, whose assumed superiority and inferiority could be attributed to the all-wise purposes of a supreme creator, served to augment the self-confidence of the whites and to allay any gnawings of guilt that they might feel. It should be noted in this connection that such highly eclectic interpretations of biblical authority enabled Christians to make moral sense of the institution of slavery.

Religious Interpretations of Social Institutions

We turn now from the consideration of the different meanings which societies, whether faced by adversity or success, have imputed to their own history, to religious interpretations of social class and of economic and political institutions. Class systems assign different and unequal statuses to a society's members. Sometimes the resulting social inequalities are not only extreme but also rigidly fixed. This situation poses the problem once more of interpreting the social system in moral and meaningful terms.

---

* It may not be out of place to mention here that many of the most ardent empire builders were the sons of English clergymen. Though these young men (like Admiral Nelson) had the spur of economic interest, they were likely to have needed a religious justification as well.

The Hindu Caste System

The Hindu caste system of ancient India, currently undergoing considerable change, is an outstanding example of the moralization of radical social inequality. The salient fact about this system is that the individual's life station, including usually his occupation, was fixed at birth and no individual effort on his part could change it. Furthermore, in assigning highest caste ranking to the Brahmins, Hindu society was granting priority within its social system to the very group whose hereditary occupation connected it most closely with the society's dominant cultural value.[8] This cultural value consisted of an exceedingly complicated religious ritual; the right to perform its most important parts was reserved for members of the Brahmin caste. The other castes* measured their social and religious distance from the Brahmins.

The Hindu caste system clearly poses a large moral problem. Why, for instance, should some lazy and possibly worthless Brahmin enjoy the greatest social prestige whereas an upright and diligent Sudra (a member of the servant caste) or an outcaste is not only segregated occupationally but also spurned socially and deprived religiously? The Hindu answer to this question—an answer giving the caste system moral justification—was found in the supernatural world. Interpretation of this answer requires some understanding of the Hindu religious outlook.

The Hindu doctrine of reincarnation, which carries the main burden of justifying the inequities of the caste system, is bound up with Hinduism's conception of the ultimate spiritual destiny of the individual. This spiritual goal is the reabsorption of his individual soul, or *atman*, with the Universal World Soul, or *Brahmā*. In the course of his journeying to this goal the individual is thought to persist through thousands of years and thousands of lives. Throughout the journey he is bound by his personal *dharma*, the relentless chain of causation set in motion by all his past actions in all his previous lives. His *kharma*, or destiny in any subsequent life or lives, is considered to be the direct result of his *dharma*. An individual is believed to be subject to the possibility of reincarnation as human being or animal, male or female, high-caste or low-caste member. According to this religious doctrine, whatever the caste position of an individual, he receives no more and no less than his just deserts earned in previous lives.

There are two striking things about this interpretation. First, it fitted extremely well the concrete conditions of Hindu society: as a justification for a rigid system of caste the religious doctrine of reincarnation seems custom made. A second significant point is the preeminently other-worldly, nonempirical character of the doctrine. Indeed, the Hindu emphasis on the attainment, through myriad lives, of an other-worldly spiritual state gave religious sanction for placing the main focus of all human striving in the super-empirical world. This had the further effect of devaluing concrete activities and engendering attitudes of indifference and apathy toward the social and economic sufferings and injustices endured by human beings in this mortal life.

---

* There were (and are) literally hundreds of castes and subcastes, not to mention unfortunate multitudes who were outside the system of caste ranking. However, only the principle of caste concerns us here.

The Class System of Medieval Europe

The medieval European system of social classes, or estates, differs in important respects from the Hindu caste system. The method by which religious thought endowed the medieval class system with moral significance also differs. Though medieval Europe, in common with ancient India, institutionalized its status differences, the latter were not as rigid or as irreversible as those of Hindu society. Furthermore the two systems embodied very different cultural values. Whereas the key cultural value of the Hindus, to which their status system was geared, was ritual proficiency, that of medieval Europeans was the possession of land. In the medieval system the relation in which the individual stood to the feudal system of land tenure more than any other single factor determined his class standing. The members of the different classes, landowners great and small, clergy, burghers, and tenants-in-villeinage were bound to one another, and thus to the society as a whole, by reason of the particular character of their relationships to the land. Each individual's relationship to the land also defined the whole gamut of his rights and obligations to his fellows.

The medieval system, then, perpetuated substantial inequalities which required moral interpretation. It may seem strange that Christianity, with its doctrinal stress on the value of every Christian soul and the equality of all sinners in the sight of God, could have succeeded in morally justifying a system of class inequality. Its explanatory task, to be sure, was not easy. One possibility was to have interpreted the equality of Christian souls in a purely spiritual sense and to have ignored earthly differences in status as religiously irrelevant. But Christian philosophy did not venture far along such an interpretative path. True, Christian creeds were explicit in the declaration of belief in a supernatural future world. In heaven, purgatory, or hell appropriate rewards and punishments for the conduct of this-worldly affairs were promised to believers. If we are to believe Dante, those who occupied the positions of greatest prestige in this world stood less chance of gaining positions of privilege hereafter than those of low estate.

Christian philosophers, however, were aware that according to orthodox Christian belief the fate of the individual soul throughout all eternity hung on the conduct of a single this-worldly life. Though the grace of God was freely offered to all, grace had to be received by the Christian in this life. Thus worldly life, related to salvation itself, was invested with a crucial value. The Christian, then, unlike the Hindu who contemplated eternity through vistas of successive incarnate lives, could not afford to regard known social arrangements as spiritually unimportant.

Accordingly, in the eyes of Christian philosophers Christian civil society, including its class system and its economic and political arrangements, was imbued with a moral purpose. St. Augustine, whose *City of God* most clearly expresses this conception of purpose, explained that the moral justification of civil society is to maintain such conditions that Christians are able to conduct their earthly lives so as to save their immortal souls. The chief agency within civil society, as Augustine saw it, which enables individuals to attain salvation is the organized Christian Church, the divinely ordained means for the dispensation of grace. Since this Church existed within the framework of a feudal society which after the collapse of the Roman Empire was the only organization capable of defending Christianity against the threats of heathens and barbarians, the whole feudal order was endowed with moral meaning. In some such terms as these medieval Christian thought gave moral meaning to the medieval class system. This religious endorsement of the class system and of civil society itself, however, was a conditional one. The arrangements of civil society were not religiously underwritten for their intrinsic merit but as the means to a supernatural objective.

Religious Interpretations of Economic and Political Systems

Economic institutions, as well as the class systems with which they are intermeshed, call for moral interpretation. The distribution of wealth and the means by which it is amassed may give rise to feelings of injustice and inequity. In the social system of ancient India we pointed out how the concrete world was strongly rejected by religion: it was regarded as māyā, or illusion. This radical rejection of the world not only devalued economic activity, but also relegated it to an unregulated moral limbo. Since material wealth and economic activity were illusory, religious thought could, so to say, wash its hands of them. The propertyless ascetic was both supported and revered, but economic exploitation of the masses and the extortion of usurers went unchecked.

The situation in medieval Europe was strikingly' different. Christian religious thought, as we have seen, assigned a moral meaning to civil society on conditional terms. It was only in the light of the other-worldly, nonempirical goals that life in this world was sanctified. The gaining of heaven was the Christian's major objective. Therefore his moral problem concerning economic activity was how to engage in it without falling into sin and so jeopardizing his chance of heaven.

In this dilemma the social objectives of wealth and economic activity were emphasized. Wealth was to be regarded as essentially for use and was neither to be hoarded nor avidly amassed. Hence usury and the taking of unfair profit were religiously condemned and attempts were made to maintain fair prices by the regulations of merchant and craft guilds. This conception of economic activity, the student of sociology should note, was not only morally but also economically appropriate in a society of poor communications, undeveloped urban life, and scarcity of monetary metals.

Furthermore medieval Christendom, in contrast to ancient India, also gave a moral interpretation to political authority. In India the village *panchayats* embodied the belief in corporate responsibility for the control of local community affairs, but the authority exercised over larger areas by rajahs and princelings was despotic, capricious, and relatively meaningless morally. Christian thought, on the other hand, which regarded political institutions as means for the Christian to pursue both his sanctified earthly purposes and his heavenly goal, interpreted political authority in moral terms. All earthly authority was assumed to be ordained by God, the Supreme Ruler of the World, and was believed to be delegated to its earthly wielders as a sacred trust. Political authority, thus religiously sanctioned, was expected to be exercised by earthly rulers for the benefit of the ruled, while dutiful obedience was required from all those lawfully subjected to it. St. Thomas Aquinas— whose writings depicted in moral terms the social and political order of medieval times more systematically than any other single contemporary— maintained that only in the most extreme cases, in which rulers through flagrant abuse of their delegated authority might be assumed to have forfeited their sacred trust, could rebellion against such authority be justified religiously.

Religion, Social Change, and Upheaval

Our discussion of ancient India and medieval Christendom has been concerned with the ways in which long-established religions gradually evolved moral interpretations of the social systems in which these religions themselves emerged. When the membership of a particular religion finally includes all or nearly all the members of a society, it is all but unavoidable that the sacred interpretation of the social order also will include moral explanation of the power structure of the society. However, this situation is likely to occur only after very many years of reciprocal interaction between the religious institutions and other social institutions. It is largely for this reason that the social systems of both ancient India and medieval Christendom displayed such a high degree of correspondence between official religious interpretations of social structure and the actual institutional arrangements. Long-established and inclusive religious interpretations of this type often encourage the maintenance of things as they are. Religiously supported conservatism can be highly repressive, to be sure, having served in both ancient and modern times to maintain tyranny. This is why Voltaire inveighed against the part played by the Church in prerevolutionary France. And in prerevolutionary Russia, as well as in contemporary Spain and Latin America, examples may be cited of a similar alliance between religious and reactionary forces.

By endorsing the status quo, then, religion not only provides social stability but sometimes supports extreme conservatism. But religion also has precisely the opposite functions at times, giving moral justification to groups which challenge strongly established social systems. (Even when such regimes are attacked in the name of antireligion or atheism, both the fervor and philosophy of the challengers are apt to have a quasi-religious quality.) The ethic of the great founded religions, in fact, contains potentially at least a revolutionary dynamic. This revolutionary ethic may remain latent in a society during the long years of the dominance of a conventionalized religion, only to reassert itself eventually as a new religious revelation to a small, dynamic group of believers. Indeed, throughout history from within established religious organizations there have been these periodic resurgences of groups dedicated to a thorough-going observance of what they believed to be a pure form of a traditional religious ethic which their society had neglected. Christianity was itself this kind of social movement within traditional Judaism, as was Buddhism within the framework of Hinduism. Examples of many such groups in more modern times will readily occur to the reader.

These resurgent groups typically are at first quite small, in their early days constituting little islands, as it were, of active faith and ethical strictness amidst the surrounding sea of the wicked social world. At first the religious ethic impresses its meaning on the group's internal social arrangements, and few compromises are made with worldly affairs. Such groups are often somewhat cut off from the wider institutional life of their societies, including the traditional organizations of religion to which they are frequently hostile. English Quakerism in the seventeenth century is a good example both of this semi-isolation and of the antagonism to the "steeple houses" of conventionally organized religion. Sooner or later, however, many though by no means all, such groups radically redefine their relationship to the outer society and, usually in conventional terms, reinterpret the moral meaning of the social order itself.

The emergence of radical religious groups coincides, as a rule, with some degree of social, economic, and political upheaval within the larger society. Moreover the numbers of resurgent religious groups are frequently, though not exclusively, recruited from those who have reason to feel themselves to be unjustly treated under the existing system of social arrangements. Revolt against established injustice, however, depends for its success on more than such practical considerations as physical strength and force of arms. For the established social system has already been given religious sanction. Thus for the challenging groups, without any moral interpretation of their own position, to attempt to overthrow the system would entail not only revolution but also sacrilege. Therefore under-privileged groups who for one reason or another feel themselves strong enough to challenge society's accepted social, economic, and political arrangements must themselves possess a compelling counterinterpretation of the meaning of society.

Of the many examples of the moralization by religion of the claims of newly emergent groups who contest the rights of established power, we select a well-known case from the history of Western society. In Western Europe, during the period between 1500 and 1800, not only were earlier institutions transformed, but their meaning was drastically reinterpreted[9] Neither the medieval religious restrictions on certain forms of economic activity, such as usury—restrictions frequently honored more often in the breach than the observance—nor the political theory of divinely constituted political authority was congenial to the aspirations of the newly rising urban and commercial classes. These groups, which by the beginning of the seventeenth century were strong enough to play an aggressive role, were in need of a powerful moral justification for their challenge to the established order.

The economic and political revolution that ushered in the modern world coincided with the religious revolt generally known as Protestantism. The term *Protestantism* is used here to include not only the churches of the Lutheran revolt, but also numerous other religious protest groups. Some of the latter, unlike Lutheranism, were both ethically and socially radical: they condemned "root and branch" the existing economic, political, and religious institutions. Among the most vital and aggressive of these new religious groups were those founded by John Calvin. He had his headquarters in the Swiss city of Geneva, which was on the way to becoming an important commercial center. It was no mere accident, then, that the people attracted to Calvin's teachings were often drawn from the urban and commercial classes who were beginning to make their way up in the world, and who were ready to demand a voice in matters political as well as religious.

We owe to the German sociologist, Max Weber, an illuminating analysis of ways in which the Calvinistic ethic encouraged the development of modern capitalism. Weber's best-known work, *The Protestant Ethic and the Spirit of Capitalism*, brings out specifically how the Calvinistic variety of Puritanism and emerging capitalism reinforced one another.[10] The English economist, R. H. Tawney, in *Religion and the Rise of Capitalism* elaborated Weber's thesis though he criticized Weber for attributing autonomy to religious factors. Whatever the validity of this appraisal, Weber's study reveals important interrelations between developments in religious thought and concurrent changes in economic and political institutions.

Calvinistic belief not only exceedingly strictly enjoined hard work and prohibited all manner of extravagance and frivolity, but it denied the validity of the ecclesiastical system for the attainment of the good life on earth and of heaven through the dispensation of sacramental grace. The duly authorized administration of this sacramental system was and is central to Catholic Christianity. Calvinist doctrine held, however, that only God knew who was saved and who was damned eternally; neither individual effort nor sacramental grace could alter His predestined purposes. The Calvinist concept of God emphasized almost exclusively His transcendent aspects, viewing Him as the Omniscient and Terrible Ruler of the Universe, the Inscrutable Dispenser of justice and doom. Whereas the medieval Christian, in thinking of the world to come, was mainly concerned with the gaining of heaven (and in this objective could rely on the help of Christ, the Virgin Mary, and the Saints as well as the entire sacramental system of the Church), the Calvinist was obsessed by an overpowering fear of hell and the dread necessity of facing his fate with a transcendent and terrible God alone.

The political correlate of Calvinism may seem obscure. An overwhelming impulse to avoid hell for themselves and to warn others of the awful danger in which they stood, instead of paralyzing Calvinists, as one might suppose, gave them a powerfully dynamic driving force. Since in their view God alone possessed the knowledge of who was saved and who was damned, they found it easy for practical purposes to think of powerful people—especially those among their religious and political rivals—as in imminent peril of doom and to regard themselves as God's elect, charged with the destiny of waging moral and physical war on the wicked rulers of the world and threatening them with both deposition and impending hell.

At the outset of this revolutionary movement Calvinist John Knox, in Scotland, trumpeted against the monstrous rule of women,* and largely due to his fulminations the autocratic and ineffective regime of the luckless Mary Queen of Scots was overthrown. A little later Holland—a tiny country whose booming commercial and financial activities typified the spirit of the new age —under the leadership of its Calvinist rulers and with the aid of a Puritan England successfully defied the ancient despotisms of France and Spain. Meanwhile in England, Calvinistic members of Parliament, spurred on by those of other independent Protestant groups, not only resisted the tyrannical government of the Stuart kings, but advanced religious justifications for radical political doctrines in which they anticipated the more extreme democratic theories of a later day. These religious enthusiasts, moreover, were ready to back up theory with force. The Puritan Cromwell, with the support of radical Protestant sectaries in the army of Ironsides, defeated Charles I in battle, beheaded him, and finally undertook to enforce the "rule of the saints with the sword."

Max Weber regards the Calvinist sects as the religious spearhead of this revolutionary movement in economic and political life. Other writers emphasize the part played by various non-Calvinistic, independent congregational

---

* The full title of Knox's famous pamphlet was *The First Blast of the Trumpet against the Monstrous Regiment of Women*, the women being Mary Queen of England; Mary of Guise, Regent of France; and Mary Queen of Scots—all Roman Catholics.

sects. Though this historical problem continues unanswered, the fact remains that resurgent religious sects succeeded in impressing much of their religious interpretation of the moral significance of political and economic institutions upon their contemporaries.

As we turn from politics to economics, we recognize the significance of the social interpretation Calvinists gave to their central doctrine of predestination. Far from inferring that since nothing a man may do will suffice to save him from hell and that therefore he may with impunity spend his life in this world in idleness and self-indulgence, they drew the rather astonishing conclusion that because no man can possibly know his other-worldly destiny he should, for the greater glory of God, live as if, in fact, he were saved. The Calvinists were taking no chances. Whatever their fate, they were duty bound to practice the virtues, notably those of industry, self-denial, and thrift. They held, too, that the exercise of these virtues should take place in the individual's occupation or calling.[11]

Weber dubbed the Calvinists "inner-worldly ascetics" because they brought to the conduct of their worldly business affairs the virtues practiced by the monks in the cloister. We can see how this harnessing of business activity with self-denying industry and thrift was productive of savings and surplus, vital essentials for capitalist investment. Moreover, just as the enterprise of a Calvinist's salvation was a lonely individual risk,[12] so also did the development of capitalist enterprise depend on risks taken by venturesome individuals.

As the Calvinists became influential, however, they faced a grave problem that all successful religious groups have had to face. As more and more people joined the Calvinistic ranks the movement could no longer regard the world as something external to itself. Furthermore, since the social and economic standing of their members was continually advancing, Calvinists could not perpetually justify their existence by contrasting their own humble virtues with the proud pretensions of evil men in power. The time came when they themselves were the men in power. Their challenge to the old order having succeeded, they were forced by this very success to evolve a moral interpretation of the meaning of not mere social challenge, but of the newly established economic and political order that they had helped to create.

The Problem of Meaning in Different Types of Societies

Thus through the ages men have sought solutions for the ultimate whys of social experience, and in these solutions they have attempted to reconcile the actualities of social systems with men's highest standards of morality and justice. Since there is an ever-present disparity between the justice meted out to people by social institutions and ideal conceptions of justice and right, there is a need for the "balancing of the moral books" in religious terms, that is, in terms transcending common sense or science.

In simpler societies, of the kind described earlier as type one, religious interpretations of the meaning of society may be implicit rather than explicit. In such societies the human group itself may constitute a sacred value for its members, and hence distinctions between ideal morality and actual customs may not always be clearly drawn. In this case the very existence of the group is its own moral justification: whatever is—simply is—is just and right. But even in these simpler societies the degree of correspondence between the ideal and the actual is relative rather than absolute.

The greater complexity of societies of type two is accompanied by larger differences between the fortunes of rich and poor, of rulers and ruled, than in societies of type one. With an increase in the division of labor, moreover, the opportunities for the exploitation of man by man are augmented, and so too, perhaps, is the total reservoir of human guilt. In the early stages of these societies emergent ethical religions enunciate codes that are in important respects challenges to encrusted custom. As these societies mature religion also serves to furnish an explanation of the meaning of society which enables the mighty to feel assured of the justice of their station while the poor and humble are kept content with their lowly estate. When in the later stages of their development these societies undergo social convulsions of various sorts and new interests challenge a former distribution of power, new outcroppings of religion provide new interpretations, which help to justify in moral terms both the challenge itself and the new social order.

In societies of type two, in which religion typically underwrites the values of the basic social institutions, the part played by religion in investing traditional institutions with moral significance stands out in clear relief. Can the same be said of the part played by religion in societies of type three, our modern industrial societies? What interpretation does religion give to the relationships of modern urban man to the state and to the economic order? What meaning does it assign to the vast network of conflicting power relationships in our shrinking world?

In these societies the injustices and inequities in the diverse fates of individuals and of nations are plain. However, secular interpretations of the meaning of the social order exist alongside religious ones. In modern industrial societies, as we pointed out earlier, secular entities, such as the nation or the state or a particular form of government, may be suffused with religious overtones. Hence nationalism, communism, and possibly democracy itself may become quasi-religions, rivals to the traditional spiritual religions of the world.

Can the interpretations of these secular religions, as they are sometimes called, suffice to invest the huge inequities of the modern world with moral meaning? History has not yet given the answer to this question. There are some who think that the moral doctrines of these secular faiths are becoming threadbare and that in this time of crisis modern societies are on the brink of evolving vast new spiritual and religious interpretations of the meaning of our world society.[13]

Footnotes to Chapter Five

1. Cf. Weber, Max: *From Max Weber: Essays in Sociology.* Translated and edited by H. H. Gerth and C. Wright Mills. New York, Oxford University Press, 1946, p. 275.
2. Cf. Parsons, Talcott: *Religious Perspectives of College Teaching in Sociology and Social Psychology,* New Haven, Edward W. Hazen Foundation, 1951, pp. 13–4.
3. *Ibid.,* p. 14.
4. Cf. Weber, Max: *op. cit.,* p. 273.
5. Barber, Bernard: "Acculturation and Messianic Movements," *American Sociological Review* 6:663–8 (Oct. 1941).
6. Weber, Max: *op. cit.,* p. 271.
7. *Ibid.,* p. 276.

8. *Ibid.*, pp. 396–7.
9. Cf. Tawney, R. H.: *Religion and the Rise of Capitalism*, New York, Harcourt, Brace & Co., 1926, pp. 65–132. (Reprinted as a Mentor Book 1948.)
10. Weber, Max: *The Protestant Ethic and the Spirit of Capitalism.* Translated by T. Parsons. London, George Allen and Unwin, 1930, pp. 35–46.
11. *Ibid.*, p. 121.
12. *Ibid.*, pp. 106–7.
13. See, for example, Sorokin, Pitirim: *The Crisis of Our Age*, New York, E. P. Dutton & Co., Inc., 1941, Chap. 9, especially pp. 322–6; and Toynbee, Arnold J.: *The Study of History*, abridgement of Vols. I–VI by D. C. Somervell, New York, Oxford University Press, 1947, pp. 544–554.

chapter six

Religious Organization

The Social and Sociological Problems of Religious Organization

An inescapable dilemma confronts all social organizations designed to mold human behavior after a prescribed pattern, whether the pattern be set by religious doctrine, ethical precept, or political philosophy. If organizations are to succeed in influencing human societies in the direction of their aims, they must be effective on a double front. On the one hand they must discipline the habits of their members in accordance with their particular ideals. On the other hand, if they also desire to influence the larger society, they must eventually expand their organization and augment their potential influence by attracting to their ranks persons of prestige and power in the world outside. These two requirements constitute the horns of a dilemma, for success on either of these fronts usually means compromise on the other. Thus religious organization is faced with the choice of maintaining its ethical and spiritual purity at the price of limiting the sphere of its social influence or if it is to exercise a dominant influence in a particular society, the price may be the sacrifice, in whole or in part, of its own distinctive ideals.

To characterize this situation as a dilemma involves two important assumptions. The first refers to the problem of maintaining group discipline, the assumption being that strict religious and ethical discipline is likely to be opposed to the behavior of most of the group members. Individuals differ in their religious capacity and interest, few being outstandingly gifted religiously or totally dedicated to religious aims. Furthermore, there can be no doubt that religious discipline, when accepted in its entirety, is exceedingly demanding. The ultimate claims of religious standards are upon the whole man. He may be asked to give up the free use of his money and time, the satisfactions of affection and family life, a secure and steady job, the pursuit of the sensual pleasures of eating, drinking, and sexuality; and more, he may be required to reorient his entire psychic world, his innermost thoughts and imaginings, his intimate desires and yearnings. A twenty-four-hour-a-day allegiance is asked of the totally committed adherent. No other type of human organization makes such a total claim, with the significant exceptions of totalitarian political organizations, which have themselves become quasi-religious.

Of course, few religions make in practice such far-reaching claims upon their members; in certain types, as we shall see, the most superficial conformity is enough. But the extremes to which the demands of religious and ethical discipline go indicate some of the difficulties, such as defection, secession, and

56

rebellion, that may beset a religious organization not composed entirely of saints if its leaders draw the disciplinary rein too tight.*

Our second assumption that refers to the problem of influencing human conduct is that the ethical aims of religious organizations usually are not consistent with the conventional aims of society and its institutions. In other words, a basic conflict exists between the religious interest and worldly society. Religious groups can meet this situation in either of two ways. They can attempt to save their members from the wicked world by withdrawing from it as far as possible. Alternatively, they can engage in active battle with the world and attempt to change it. (In modern times, for example, the Plymouth Brethren have taken the former path, whereas Jehovah's Witnesses have taken the latter.) Those groups which withdraw usually remain small and exercise a rather slight influence on the larger society.** The militantly propagandist groups, on the other hand, can bring their influence to bear upon the world outside only if they expand their ranks. If this expansion is to achieve the ends of the group in question, however, it must include at least some members of power and prestige in the society concerned. Thus Christianity which at first comprised relatively obscure individuals became the dominant religion of the Roman Empire itself, with consequent power to influence its institutions only when it enlisted individuals of high standing, including finally the Emperor Constantine.

The dilemma lies in the fact that this expansion with its increasing capacity to influence society is achieved at the cost of dilution. In the course of its growth in numbers and power the religious organization comes to include at least some elements which it has been combating. Thus a part, at least, of the formerly sinful world no longer excluded is integrated with the religious organization. Therefore the religious struggle with the world outside has to be waged not only with external foes but also within the social arena of the organization itself. The religious organization as it grows in responsibility and social influence incorporates the entire range of worldly problems: problems of policy and of government, of leadership and ambition, and of the amassing of wealth, its use, distribution, and control. Hence religion in its organizational aspects—and here we are not concerned with its supernatural side—is marked by the same human problems as social life in general.[1]

Keeping in mind the limitations of all human institutions, the sociologist J. M. Yinger has sought to find a theoretical point of maximum effectiveness for religious organizations.[2] In his opinion this point would be most nearly reached when an organization had grown in numbers and power sufficiently to exert a strong social influence without having abandoned its essential ethical

---

* Certain severe types of discipline would seem hardly feasible for large groups of men and women in daily contact with the ordinary demands of the workaday world. It was perhaps for this reason that the Lord Buddha ordained two sets of rules, one for full-time Buddhist monks and a less stringent set for part-time lay followers. Almost two thousand years later St. Francis of Assisi developed two rules for the Franciscan Order, one for the friars who took the full vows and another for the famous Third Order of Franciscans, that is, men and women associated with the Order who continued to live out their lives in the world.

** We do not wish to imply, however, that withdrawing organizations, such as the medieval monasteries, have no influence on the outer world or, for that matter, that the more active group places no emphasis on the individual's salvation from the world. The difference in relative emphasis nevertheless is significant.

and religious ideals. Could both these ends be achieved fully and simultaneously there would be no dilemma, of course. But Yinger contend? that the chances of gaining the ideal balance are increased either if a large influential organization can remain sufficiently flexible to retain a place for a variety of smaller groups, strong in religious discipline and fervor, to act as a spiritual leaven or if a relatively small but intensive organization can maintain its own ethical purity but at the same time devise methods to extend its influence in the world. In Yinger's opinion, with which neither author nor readers need concur, the Catholic Church in the thirteenth century most nearly approached maximum effectiveness by following the first alternative, whereas the twentieth-century Society of Friends approximates this goal by following the second one.

Many thoughtful and even religious-minded people sometimes feel disillusioned with the organizational side of religion; therefore we began our discussion of religious organization with a statement of its central, inescapable problem. We made a clear-cut distinction between religion conceived of as an individual's relation to God and the ultimate objects of his faith and religion as a human institution, and indicated sociology's most important insight, namely that since institutional religion is human it is subject to all the conditions that limit human organization in general.

Religion as human organization is thus subject to imperfection, change, and flux. We can look neither to the past nor to the future for the perfect religious institution that never changes and never fails. Important as religious organization has been, and still is, not only as a stabilizing force in society but also as a source of security for its members, it is itself only relatively stable. The history of organized Protestant Christianity bears abundant testimony to the truth of this statement; and even the Roman Catholic Church, a religious institution of outstanding stability, has undergone many transformations in the course of its long history.[3]

We need not be surprised, then, that religious organization is not completely perfect or permanent, nor disillusioned at the inevitable discrepancy between religion's lofty ethical ideals and their embodiment in human institutions. The sociological knowledge that all institutions are the result of willed human activity and that consequently there is no automatic correspondence between noble ideals and institutional forms should temper both disillusionment and defeatism. Furthermore as sociologists we know that no single organization, religious or otherwise, is the only force at work in a society, hence what any one organization can accomplish depends to a great extent on the strength of the other institutions and on the counterforces and trends of change at work. Thus the student of sociology, if he is a member of a religious organization, will be wise to limit his demands for purely organizational achievement. It is open to him, however, since human organizations are molded by human action, to exert whatever influence he may have to help his own church to come closer to its avowed ideal. His sociological understanding of the organizational structure of which he is a part and of his own status within it should assist him in this task. These comments are not to be interpreted as a sort of Pollyanna endorsement by sociology of the imperfections of religious organization. Sociology as a science is concerned neither with endorsement nor its opposite, but with accurate description and analysis. The thinking individual must take responsibility for his own course of action.

Moreover when as students we try to understand the actual historical development of particular churches—including much evil perpetrated by them under religion's cloak—we are confronted with a strange paradox. For anti-institutional trends exist at the heart of religious organization itself. This fact derives from the circumstance that religion has its other-worldly as well as this-worldly interests and concerns. Hence churches, unlike purely secular organizations, must somehow find room for both. Many great religious teachers have supplied a sort of running critique of religious organization, especially when the latter, deadened by formalism or corrupted by power, has stifled the expression of religion's other-worldly ends.

These religious leaders, such as Moses, Buddha, Jesus, and Mohammed, or in more modern times men like St. Francis, George Fox, and Roger Williams, have usually had something of the mystic about them. Mysticism—that communication between the religious believer and the ultimate objects of his faith—as experienced within the consciousness of the worshipper is an aspect of religious experience that has proved highly resistant to organization. Furthermore, persons in whom the mystical other-worldly side of religion predominates have rarely proved entirely amenable to this-worldly organizational control.* It is hardly accidental that the great religious teachers mentioned above were highly critical of the official religious organization of their times. Such leaders have at times disrupted existing institutions while providing inspiration for new ones. In spite of the dilemma in which all religious organization is involved, one of its outstanding features is its abundant capacity to renew itself from within. This polar tension between other-worldly and this-worldly, radical and conservative, tendencies endows religious organization with its inherent vitality and, moreover, makes it a fascinating and exceedingly complicated study for the sociologist.

Changing Forms of Religious Organization

The basic dilemma of religious organization may be seen more concretely when we consider one of its main manifestations, namely the religious movement. A religious movement here refers to any organized attempt to spread a new religion or a new interpretation of an already existing religion. The great world religions of Buddhism, Christianity, and Islam can be regarded as the outcome of religious movements. Similarly, religious movements also develop within the framework of already established religions, for example, the Franciscan and the Protestant movements within Catholic Christianity, the Oxford Movement within Anglicanism, and Father Divine's Peace Mission within

---

* The mystic and the mystic element in religion possibly just because they are never entirely amenable to organization point up some of its basic problems. Mystics, however, are by no means always organizational rebels or founders of new religious movements. True, the thorough-going mystic is potentially an anarchist as far as organization is concerned, for in the final analysis there is for him no authority higher than his own inner light. The mystic, however, is frequently not so much against religious organization as indifferent to it. Some of them have been hermits and solitaries, such as St. Simeon Stylites on his famous pillar. Others have formed their own independent communities. Still others have remained peacefully in the fold of established religious organizations, organizations as different from one another as East European Jewry, the Society of Friends, and the Roman Catholic Church. However amenable they may be to organizational discipline in matters of indifference to them, yet, as an English bishop once said, "You can never quite tell where you are with a person who claims to be guided by the Inner Light." For a socially aroused mystic may turn into a dynamo of energy and play hob with the stabilized smugness of established religious organizations.

American Protestantism. Such movements typically pass through a series of rather well-defined stages and after their initial expansive phases usually become stabilized in relation to other religions. The more settled phases of such religious movements may themselves furnish the matrix from which later religious movements arise.

The first phase of a religious movement is dominated by the personality of its founder. Whatever the quality of his religious insight, a successful founder possesses a power of fascination, a compelling attraction, that draws men to him. This essential attribute is sometimes called charisma.* Though founders of religious movements are often critical of existing religious organization, their own religious and ethical message, however new in certain respects, inevitably owes much to the religious tradition in which the particular founder has been nurtured. Thus the teachings of Jesus are both critical of organized Judaism and yet grounded in it, and the message of Buddha is at once a revolt against traditional Hinduism and yet deeply molded by it.

During its early formative years the movement has a fluid, informal primary-group character. Groups of first-followers, whether of Jesus of Nazareth, Buddha, Mohammed, or St. Francis of Assisi, comprise small circles of individual adherents who stimulate one another, while being stimulated themselves, by face-to-face contact with their charismatic leader. This contact supplies for them both cohesion and dynamic. Moreover, such "circular" fellowships commonly generate enormous psychic and social energy.** The group's main problem (in this innovating, creative phase), is not organization as such, but rather to absorb and to gain a hearing for the new religious teachings. To be sure, as such groups begin to grow their founders may supply them with a rule of life and conduct, such as Jesus' instructions to the twelve and to the seventy or Buddha's enunciation of the Noble Eightfold Path. Yet matters of rules and discipline are not usually crucial at this stage. Few precise, intellectual answers are given to questions about the nature of the founder and the authority for his mission—though such questions almost always arise. Similarly, while the leader lives and his presence dominates his followers the delegation of his authority and the relative ranking of individuals within the movement are unlikely to become burning issues.

In the second phase of the movement the successors of the founder are forced to resolve and clarify important matters pertaining to organization, belief, and ritual that were left in abeyance during the founder's lifetime. At this stage the movement typically becomes what we now term a church: the formal organization of a group of worshippers who share common and defined beliefs and rituals concerning the sacred objects and entities they revere. In this second phase, which is often precipitated by the advent of a second generation of believers, qualifications for membership are made more explicit and the lines of authority in the organization are more sharply drawn. Moreover, beliefs about the sacred person and mission of the founder are formulated as official theologies and creeds and a cult of the founder involving formal

---

* This term, used by the German sociologist of religion, Max Weber, is applicable not only to religious but also to political leaders. Adolf Hitler is an example of a charismatic leader.

** The germ cells of both Hitlerism and Communism are good examples of the dynamic energy of such charismatically led political groups.

acceptance of the beliefs embodied in such creeds not infrequently supersedes a more spontaneous, personal adherence to his teachings. Furthermore, religious practices, such as the Christian celebration of the Last Supper and the Hebrew Passover, gradually develop into formally prescribed rituals. This second stage is often accompanied by struggles over leadership, such as those that rent Islam after the death of Mohammed or conflict concerning the formulation of beliefs, such as those that shook Christianity in the second and third centuries A.D. To resolve such struggles a "second founder" is sometimes required. In such circumstances Christianity produced the organizing genius, Paul of Tarsus, and Islam, the Caliph Omar.

If a movement successfully survives the second stage, the third is characteristically one of continued expansion and diversification. The movement becomes established and takes on a variety of organizational forms. Religious movements differ in the degree to which they expand, some remaining delimited by ethnic, class, and cultural barriers. Buddhism, Christianity, and Islam transcended these barriers and in addition made converts of individuals of outstanding political and economic power. At this stage a religious movement confronts the danger of becoming the victim of its own success, and here we come face to face with the organizational dilemma discussed in the first section of this chapter.

This third stage, which may be protracted in time, poses another problem. The leaders now have the task of answering why, in spite of the movement's success in gaining followers, its original objectives, so immediate and vivid to the first disciples, have not yet been achieved in concrete fact. This problem is especially acute for those movements with an apocalyptic message, whose leaders have alerted their followers for the imminent second coming of a messiah, for the end of the world and the establishment, by supernatural means, of a heavenly kingdom on earth. With the advent of the third generation of Christians, for example, it became necessary to provide an additional interpretation of Christ's second coming—an interpretation which stressed His coming in the sacraments and His invisible presence in the hearts of the faithful—and necessary to transfer the hope for the establishment of God's Kingdom to a distant, other-worldly future.

With the exception of Judaism,* which never entirely abandoned its hope for the tangible restoration of Jerusalem, few religions have held steadily as their objective the establishment of an earthly Kingdom of God. The recent emphasis on what is known as the *social gospel* among some Christian groups is one modern attempt to implement this objective. But it has been left to the great so-called political religions of our own day, such as Fascism, Marxism, and Communism, to make the social embodiment of their particular version of heaven on earth their official, primary aim. These political-religious movements, however, have now entered their third stage, and their leaders, too, have been faced with difficult problems of reinterpreting objectives when their attainment has been unduly delayed. With these reinterpretations the leaders justify both their own dominance and the continued existence of the move-

---

* Judaism, of course, has always had and still has today spiritual, as well as tangible, objectives. There has persisted in Judaism a trend, however, strikingly exemplified in Zionism in our own day, to pin the hope of religious fulfilment to a particular people and a particular place.

ments. For at this third stage of their development both religious and political movements have an established interest in their own continuance, which becomes a major objective of their organizations.

Types of Religious Organization and Types of Society

All students of religious organization are deeply indebted to the writings of the German scholar, Ernst Troeltsch, author of the monumental study, *Social Teachings of the Christian Churches*. Troeltsch distinguishes between two main types of religious group—the church and the sect. Since we have already used the term church in a general sense to characterize all forms of religious group life, we shall here, for the sake of clarity, substitute for it the Latin word *ecclesia*.[4] For Troeltsch the church, or ecclesia, is a type of religious organization characteristic of a religious movement in its mature, established phase. A sect, on the other hand, marks the early dynamic stages of a movement. Troeltsch confined his studies to Christianity. Because of the wide range of organizational types which it comprises and also because Christianity is familiar to most of us, we propose to follow his example. On the other hand the pioneer researches of Max Weber in ancient Judaism and in the religions of India and of China suggest that Troeltsch's typology is capable of a wider application.

We propose, therefore, to discuss and to amplify Troeltsch's typology and then to suggest some of the possible interrelations between these types of religious group and the three types of human society we have discussed earlier.

Although Troeltsch's ecclesia, or church-type, and the sect-type are the two main varieties of religious groups and it is useful to regard these two as polar opposites, we shall nevertheless follow those sociologists who add two further subtypes, namely the denomination and the cult.[5]

Ecclesia, Sect, Denomination, and Cult

The *ecclesia* is a church which stresses its universality within a given territory, either national or international. All members born within this given territory are considered, by virtue of their residence, to be members of the ecclesia. Its patterns of authority are typically both formal and traditional. This authority is centralized and hierarchical and hence is relayed from top to bottom of the organization by means of a chain of command. Various kinds of leaders exist in this large, diversified organization, the most typical leader being the priest rather than the prophet. The priest is an official whose authority is sanctioned by the hierarchy. His main function, namely to administer the sacramental means of grace to the members, is both exclusive and crucial.

The ecclesia, in marked distinction to the sect, neither withdraws from the world nor fights it. Its aim is rather to control the world in the interests of the organization. Hence there is close reciprocation between the government of the ecclesia and the secular institutions of the society, including civil government. For this reason, as Troeltsch has well put it, the ecclesia dominates the world and is itself dominated by it.

The ideal type of ecclesia—a universal world church—has, of course, never existed. The Catholic Church in the thirteenth century, perhaps its nearest approximation, did not include even all of Western Christendom. Today the Roman Catholic Church still exemplifies, in theory, an international ecclesia, and similarly the Anglican and Lutheran Churches furnish examples of national ecclesiae.

The *sect*, in contrast, is typically a small, exclusive group whose members join voluntarily, usually as adults. Authority is exercised by virtue of personal charisma rather than hierarchical sanction, yet nevertheless religious discipline is rigorous, and is commonly enforced by the mutual scrutiny of the group members. Sects are characterized by religious and ethical fervor, their beliefs stress primitive gospel teachings, and their practices emphasize the way of life of the early Christians. Sectarian beliefs and practices sharpen the distinction between the small, closely knit group of sect members and the outside world. Indeed, sectarians are usually hostile to members of all other churches, and often to those of rival sects. "Come out from among them and be ye separate" might well be the motto of the sect. Hence sects also tend to be radical in their rejection of secular government; sect members may, for instance, refuse to bear civil office, to perform military service, to take oaths, and to pay taxes.

Sects are of two main varieties: withdrawing sects and militant sects. The monastic orders were the principal withdrawing sects of medieval times, whereas in the modern world sects of this type include the Plymouth Brethren and the Old Order Amish of rural Pennsylvania. Among the militant sects may be numbered the Anabaptists of the seventeenth century and, though possibly less militant, the Jehovah's Witnesses of our own day.

A *denomination* is a relatively stabilized group, often of considerable size and complexity, which recruits its members largely by birthright. It is characteristically one among a number of churches within a given territory or within a number of given territories. Authority in a denomination is sometimes hierarchical in nature, and sometimes stems from the elective action of local congregations. Its discipline, unlike that of the sect, is on the whole formal and conventional rather than fervid and exacting. Its priests and pastors are usually temperate in their evangelical zeal and hold themselves chiefly responsible for the welfare of their own congregations. The denomination neither withdraws from, fights, nor controls the world, but for the most part cooperates with it. As a rule it also cooperates with the civil authorities and with most other religious bodies.

Denominations are of two main kinds. They may be one-time sects, tamed and matured, that have made their peace with the world. Or they may be former ecclesiae, which have been forced to accept denominational status as the condition of their survival in societies like the United States, where the constitution prohibits an established church of any kind. The Methodist and Baptist Churches are well-known examples of denominations that have evolved from former sects, whereas the Episcopal and Lutheran Churches—though nationally established, if modified, ecclesiae in England and Sweden respectively—are denominations in the United States.

The *cult* is a type of small religious group in some respects similar to the sect, though unlike the sect its membership is largely confined to dwellers in metropolitan areas. Ancient Athens and ancient Rome were riddled with cults no less than London, New York, and Los Angeles today. Cult members are frequently rootless urban individuals who may embrace a cult when they are confronted with loneliness and frustration in middle and later life. Thus cult members, like sect members, are voluntary joiners. But joining a cult does not imply the acceptance of group discipline. In the cult authority is at a minimum. Members may join a cult not because they accept all of its beliefs and practices, but rather because some of them happen to fit in with their own. Furthermore, membership in a cult is not exclusive, and need not debar individuals from membership in other, perhaps more conventional, churches. Thus the individual's commitment to the cult is more tenuous and the term of his membership likely to be more transient, than in a sect. Cult organization is therefore frequently loose and amorphous.

Cult leadership is charismatic, informal, often precarious, and, under metropolitan conditions of relative anonymity, sometimes corrupt. Cult beliefs frequently emphasize one particular aspect of Christian teaching, such as spiritual healing, or they may blend Christian beliefs with beliefs borrowed from other cultures, often oriental ones. Cult beliefs are usually more esoteric and mystical than the plain gospel teachings stressed by the typical sect.

Cult members as a rule neither withdraw from the world nor are they likely to be in militant opposition to it. Indeed, cultists, with some notable exceptions, are unlikely to be actively concerned with broader political and social issues. The function of the cult is rather to help its members to adjust as happily as possible to the world and its institutions.

Religious Organization and Religious Movements

Although it is possible for different types of religious organizations to exist together within a single society, nevertheless some types of church are more congenial to certain types of society than to others.

Historical evidence indicates that new religious movements are best able to make a lasting imprint on human societies if they are born when civilizations are in turmoil. The great pre-Christian religious movements emerged during times of rapid change and upheaval which shook the early civilizations. It is a remarkable fact that roughly the same period—the seventh to the fifth centuries B.C.—saw the development of Confucianism in China, of philosophical Brahminism and the beginnings of Buddhism in India, and the prophetic movement in Judea, to say nothing of the emergence of classical culture in Greece. This period was a time of unsettlement—in some respects comparable to our own—across the whole civilized world.[6] In this age the great religious movements were born and, largely due to religion's influence, values which have since guided civilization took shape.

Christianity, which in many respects may be regarded as a synthesis of the Hebrew and Greek traditions, arose in a similar situation in which society and human values were in flux. The Jewish people were undergoing the difficult adjustment of absorption in the Roman Empire, which itself was in process of a transformation that eventually led to its decay. Indeed, Christianity might well have perished had not Roman imperial society, decadent as it was, manifested a great deal of individualism and tolerance. The Roman society within which Christianity emerged as a cultlike sect was in many ways comparable to the rapidly changing metropolitan societies that we have classified as type three.

The decline of Roman civilization ushered in a new type of society closely approximating that earlier characterized as type two. Thus Christianity, in common with the other great world religions, grew to maturity in a type two society, and played an important part in molding its values. In such large-scale agricultural societies the absence of nationalism and strong central government and the paucity of scientific and economic techniques enabled the church to play a dominant social and political role. Poor communications and low standards of literacy, moreover, were societywide, and by limiting competition from rival faiths, also furthered the development of an ecclesia or universal church.

When type two societies begin to break up and new classes and new interests challenge the established order, as we saw in the last chapter, a multitude of sects emerge. The established ecclesia in these societies is not only strong by virtue of its own organization, but is also a powerful supporter of the existing social and political institutions. Hence opposition to be effective must be both fervent and vigorous. Moreover, in a partially urbanized society as yet neither cosmopolitan nor highly secularized it is almost inevitable that this growing opposition to entrenched power be justified as a reversion to what may be called *gospel Christianity*. This type of religious justification was in fact employed by the fighting sectarians who flourished in seventeenth-century Europe at a time of general unrest that gave these religious groups an unrivaled opportunity to impress their particular ethic on the surrounding society. Indeed, the stamp of this Puritan ethic, in spite of all that has happened since, has not been entirely eradicated from either English or American national life.

As seventeenth-century conditions gradually gave place to those of the modern world, as societies of type two changed into those of type three, many of the earlier sects had achieved worldly success and had consequently become more stabilized and less militant. Whereas the earlier stages of the religious revolt had drastically curtailed the universal sway of that great international ecclesia, the Catholic Church, in the later stages the success of the sectaries in establishing themselves was bought at the expense of the universality of national ecclesiae, for example, the Church of England. Though there was a tendency for sects to become "tamed" as a result of their members' worldly success, nevertherless newer and more uncompromising sects continued to arise as rebellious offshoots from their parent bodies. Splintering and proliferation are characteristic tendencies of sects.

The whole complex of social conditions which favored nationalism and industrialism, as well as religious toleration, was unfavorable to the ecclesia. In our modern societies no new ecclesiae have been born. The voluntary denomination may be regarded as the most characteristic type of religious organization in type three societies. When secular governments do not endorse religious uniformity, religious affiliation becomes largely a matter of individual choice, a choice, however, which is frequently influenced by status considerations. To such conditions the denomination, a relatively large and stable yet voluntary type of religious organization, is well adapted. Moreover, such a type of organization can readily be evolved by maturing sects. Indeed, it well suits the needs of a predominantly middle-class membership which may ramify widely throughout large-scale national societies.

So well established are denominations today that it is easy to forget their sectarian beginnings. The frontier society of the United States has not only been a fertile breeding ground for sects, but has been the scene of their rapid passage to denominational status as pioneers' clearings grew into settled communities. The annals of both Baptists and Methodists illustrate this swift transition, which at times took place within the lifetime of a single preacher. Some of these doughty backwoods preachers, such as Peter Cartwright, lived to look back nostalgically on informal warm-hearted meetings in settlers' cabins. Such preachers were not thereafter quite at home in settled communities, with their brick churches and their organ music, and in buildings in which orderly rows of pews seated a citified congregation who might look to them in vain for a learned sophisticated sermon.[7]

In spite of this tendency for sects to develop into denominations, the sect is by no means extinct in societies of type three. H. Richard Niebuhr[8] and Liston Pope[9] have shown convincingly how continued social mobility has been a factor in stimulating the growth of new splinter sects. In his *Millhands and Preachers* Pope describes how, among the more prosperous sect members in a North Carolina textile town, there existed a trend for successful sects to develop into denominations. His most interesting finding, however, is that in each of these churches there were some members who did not share in the upward mobility of the dominant majority, and that it was typical for these nonmobile members to secede and to initiate new "primitive" sects. Unable to share in the improved social standing of their more successful neighbors they were unwilling to submit themselves to liturgical forms of worship, to listen to an "educated" sermon by a professional minister, and in short to have their own spontaneous spiritual exuberance curbed.

Another reason for the persistence of sects in modern secular societies is the uneven incidence of urbanization coupled with the fact of large-scale rural-urban migration. For some rural areas in type three societies remain in many respects akin to societies of type two, in which, as we observed earlier, the church typically plays a dominant social role.

People migrating from rural areas into large cities, however, frequently find themselves lost and ill at ease in a large, impersonal city church, even though it may well be a church of their own denomination. For they find it does not fulfil the same needs met by the church back home. Hence rural migrants, particularly those in low-rent urban areas, frequently form new sects or join existing ones, partly in order to gain a standing for themselves in their new environment, and partly to recapture some of the more intimate primary-group atmosphere of the rural church.

An interesting type of church emerging in the metropolitan areas of societies of type three is the cult. The metropolis mingles people and ideas from all over the world in a large-scale, impersonal type of society. Here exists a great variety of competing, and even incompatible, ethical standards and culture models; moreover the degree of anonymity means that group control of the individual is minimized. A man's work-mates may know nothing and care less for his home life, his church affairs, or his recreational activities. Similarly his wife may know little of his life at the workbench or his leisure-time cronies. Social life becomes atomized and the individual is frequently rudderless and confused. As Durkheim has put it, a condition of *anomie*, or normlessness, prevails.

Extensive anomie is a fertile breeding ground for new types of religious organization. The church historian George La Piana, in his study *Foreign Groups in Rome during the First Centuries of the Empire*, has shown how the contacts and conflicts of the foreign groups in the tenement quarters of Rome's vast immigrant areas furnished a haven for a great variety of cults and oriental mystery religions. His descriptions remind us of immigrant areas in New York or Chicago, with their converted down-at-heel brownstone houses, many of which are meeting places for Rosicrucians, spiritual or oriental churches, or more ephemeral cults. According to La Piana, one of the reasons that Christianity—itself a mystical oriental import to the Roman scene—survived and flourished while vast numbers of contemporary cults and mystery religions became extinct was that Christianity possessed a superior type of organization.[10] Christianity, in fact, had known how to profit from proximity to Rome's organizing genius. In the modern American metropolis, as in Rome, there are many cults which spring up and flourish briefly, only to wither and die. Those which survive are likely to have had at their core a relatively strong organization and to have developed it along current American denominational lines.

Christian Science (official name: Church of Christ, Scientist), for example, was in its beginnings a rather typical cult. In some respects it was an outgrowth of early metropolitan Boston, the one-time "hub of the universe"—the center of New England transcendalism. Christian Science was cultic, too, in its emphasis on a particular aspect of Christian teaching, namely spiritual healing, and also in its borrowing of cosmopolitan and oriental ideas, particularly the concept of the unreality of matter and of evil. Mary Baker Eddy, however, was a dynamic leader and organizer, and in part because of her influence and also because of the upward social mobility of Christian Scientists, this group has developed many ecclesia-like tendencies. Today it is a highly centralized, authoritarian denomination. Its typical habitat, however, still remains either the urban center or citified suburbs.

Theosophy, Anthroposophy, Bahai, Psychiana, the "I Am" movement, and the numerous spiritualist churches are all examples of successful modern cults. Whereas the struggling fly-by-night cults of the slum areas are recruited from ethnic minorities and from the underprivileged, the established cults appeal rather to the middle classes, frequently meeting in rented halls in downtown buildings—New York's Steinway Hall, for example—and begin to develop more or less centralized organizational affiliations. Successful cults, moreover, often use the latest promotional techniques of the secular society, from newspaper and mail-order advertising to radio and television programs.

Thus in societies of type three, although the denomination is the most usual form of church organization, yet sects and cults still persist, as well as modified versions of the older ecclesia. But in these societies the dominant influence of the secular institutions of government and economic life deprive organized religion of effective power to mold social institutions.* Rather it reflects them.

Forms of Local Church Organization

So far we have been concerned with broad and general aspects of the interrelationship between the organization of religion and the organization of society. We shall now consider briefly some of the main forms of church government and their repercussions on church life on the local, congregational level—where church life is experienced by the vast majority of worshippers. It is here, if anywhere, that the religious objectives of the organization become tangible in the lives of the membership and influence the social life of local communities.

There are three main types of church government: the episcopal, the pres-

---

* The influence of religious tradition is still something to be reckoned with, but we are here concerned with the organizational aspects of religion.

byterian, and the congregational. Each of these types involves a particular set
of consequences for social relationships within the church group.

The *episcopal* form of government sets the tone for the relationship between
the parish priest and his congregation by making his appointment dependent
upon episcopal choice and sanction and by subjecting him to episcopal discipline. In certain respects it is true that the priest's dependence upon the episcopate limits his initiative in local matters, yet his position as an officer of a
central organization frees him from too binding a dependence upon the wishes
and whims of a local congregation. This fact ensures considerable liberty in
the performance of his pastoral function. On the other hand, the autonomy
of the local congregations is limited by this type of arrangement. The laity
have the power of protest rather than the full right of initiative.

This form of government may be most clearly seen in churches of the
ecclesia type, but it also obtains in some denominations, notably the Methodist Episcopal Church in the United States. Methodist church government,
however, is a hybrid, combining, like the United States government itself,
strong centralized authority at the top with considerable autonomy at the
bottom.

The *presbyterian* form of organization places the main control in the hands
of the presbytery, or body of preachers, which in principle is an aristocracy
stressing educational competence. The endorsement of this organization enhances the authority of the preacher vis-à-vis his congregation, even though
it subjects him to the control of his top-ranking colleagues. On the other hand
the congregation, which is also subject to the aristocratic control of the elders,
has the right to request the appointment of a preacher. Moreover the elders
of the congregation have the right to choose, often on the basis of a kind of
preaching contest, from among the candidates who present themselves.*
These elders are not only zealous in scrutinizing preachers, both prospective
and actual, but exercise energetic sway over the rank and file of the membership. Indeed, in this type of organization it is possible for the preacher to be
caught between two fires. Nevertheless, presbyterianism, by exalting the function of the preacher and at the same time subjecting him to toughening pressures from both above and below, often succeeds in producing—among those
who survive—dominant ministerial leaders.

The *congregational* type of church, as exemplified by the early Baptists and
other independent congregations, maximizes the power of the local group in
both the choice and control of the minister and in the conduct of all organizational affairs. With the power of the central organization nonexistent (or at
a minimum) the dependence of the minister, both financial and otherwise,
on the members of the immediate congregation is at a maximum. In theory
in this type of government the congregation is itself organized democratically
and gives to all members considerable power of initiative. This initiative may
be exercised today more commonly by individuals who have the right to make
suggestions but make them through the medium of many committees and
suborganizations.

The minister thus becomes a democratic leader of a congregation which

* Some readers may be familiar with the old Scottish story about the conference held
by two elders who had just listened to the preaching of a ministerial candidate. "Ay, ay,"
said the first, "he preached a rare powerful sermon." "Ay, ay," replied the second, "But
his firrrrst prayer clean damned him."

may in fact consist of a congeries of subassociations. Hence congregational control over the conduct of the minister may be exercised through a complex of interlocking and not always harmonious groups. In addition this control may be extremely constricting, unless the congregation in question is concerned to extend the democratic principle to include the freedom of the pulpit as well as the freedom of the pew. Lacking the possibility of citing the authority or enlisting the aid of a central organization, the local congregational minister is on his own, to sink or swim, as far as his relationships with his local church is concerned. Moreover in actual practice the effective control in such an organization may not be completely democratic, since there is a tendency for the more substantial members, who pay the piper, to call the tune. Such a situation is not unknown in some of the older New England Unitarian Churches.

L. M. Smith has recently studied some differences in the quality of the relationships between minister and congregation in episcopal type churches as compared with congregational type churches. Smith questioned a sample group of some twenty episcopal and twenty congregational ministers about the reasons they had moved from one church (within their own denomination) to another. Though both groups of ministers mentioned most frequently the desire for a better position or a wider sphere of influence, it is significant that the congregational ministers cited more often the decision to leave because of tension or difficulty with organized groups of church members. On the whole, their terms of service with each congregation were somewhat shorter than those of the episcopal clergy.[11]

For the sake of clarity we have described these three forms of church government as separate, distinct types. In our contemporary society, however, all three forms are being modified to a great extent. In the episcopal churches, not excluding the Roman Catholic Church itself, since there is no longer a sufficiency of gilt-edged endowments, the enhanced financial powers of the laity have gained for them both hearing and representation, including increasing powers of initiative in affairs other than financial. In the Anglican churches in some areas committees of the laity have a limited choice, or at least a power of veto, in the selection of their priests. In part due to the influence of corresponding changes in civil government the tendency has been to democratize the episcopate and to grant a greater measure of autonomy to the local churches.

Similar tendencies have been at work to modify presbyterian forms in a democratic direction. The congregational form, on the other hand, has developed associations of local churches on a nationwide basis. This trend has also been typical of Jewish congregations, no less than of Baptist, Unitarian, and other Christian community churches. Indeed, the isolated, detached congregation appears to be ill-adapted for survival in societies of type three. Though in the associations and federations that increasingly bind these congregational churches together much care has been taken to safeguard the reserve powers of the local constituent bodies, both ministers and members feel that some degree of centralization of financial and other resources—for example, facilities for ministerial education—is of great benefit to the local churches themselves. In this development of cooperation between a federated government and local bodies the churches are in line with nationwide trends in the joint federal-local handling of education and social welfare.

The Influence of Organized Religion Today

Earlier in this chapter we stated that in modern secular societies churches reflect, rather than mold, their social surroundings. This statement should not be taken to mean that Christian denominations make no attempt to influence their national and local communities in accordance with the Christian ideal. On the contrary, in pulpit pronouncements and in philanthropic and other activities much effort is expended. The question remains, however, as to just how effective these efforts are in modifying the social scene.

In order to understand the nature of the impact made by the churches in modern communities it is helpful to examine some of the ways in which social pressures operate within individual congregations. In a study conducted in the later 1930's of the opinions on social issues of both clergy and laity in the Baltimore area a number of questions were asked designed to discover to what extent each respondent either supported or resisted certain specified suggested changes in the status quo.[12] A definite attempt was made in the questions to suggest changes that were in line with the Christian ethic. The responses of most of the clergymen to these questions showed them to be, as a group, "a little left of center." Differences between clergy in episcopal as opposed to clergy in congregational types of organization were almost negligible. The most significant differences were found to be those between clergy and laity in all types of church. Furthermore, whereas the general body of the laity tended to be only somewhat more conservative than the clerical group, the members of boards of trustees and other financial and policy-making officers of these churches were markedly more resistant to the suggested changes than were the clergy interrogated. Thus the separation between those who favored a safe conservatism and those who desired more progressive and, presumably, more Christian social policies was a cleavage within the membership of the individual local congregations.

Though we must not give undue weight to a single exploratory study involving a limited number of cases, it may afford us some insights. It at least suggests some clues as to why, in our contemporary society, pronouncements by clerical bodies, such as Episcopal synods or federal councils of churches, are commonly so much more outspoken in support of policies to promote changes in the current social order than might have been expected from the stand made by their constituent members, as individual clergymen, in their own local congregational setting. For if the clergy wish to maintain a position of influence in their own congregations—a position which in turn depends at least in part on the support of the influential laity—they are almost inevitably driven to compromise or to silence on certain social issues. Dr. Arthur Swift has said that it takes most clerical neophytes about five years to find for themselves a middle ground on which they can retain a modicum of social idealism and the necessary minimum of congregational support.[13] They may justify to themselves any compromises involved by reflecting that both rich and poor alike have souls to be saved, and that the building of Christian character rather than the promotion of this or that social program is a church's main concern.

It is far from our intention to disparage this point of view; indeed, there is very much to be said for it. It is, as we have already seen, the typical reaction of the churchly denomination. Nevertheless, the fact that this out look is rather commonly held by the most influential religious denominations is possibly one reason why modern churches—whatever other purposes they may serve for their membership and in their local communities—are not usually dynamic forces for the initiation of social change in either national or local communities.

Footnotes to Chapter Six

1. Cf. Parsons, Talcott: *Religious Perspectives*, New Haven, Edward W. Hazen Foundation, 1951, p. 27.
2. Yinger, John M: *Religion and the Struggle for Power*, Durham, N.C., Duke University Press, 1946, p. 23.
3. Parsons, Talcott: *op. cit.*, pp. 27–9.
4. Troeltsch, Ernst: *Social Teachings of the Christian Churches*, Translated by O. Wyon. New York, The Macmillan Company, 1931, pp. 333–343.
5. Von Wiese, Leopold, and Howard Becker: *Systematic Sociology*, New York, John Wiley & Sons, Inc., 1932, pp. 624–8.
6. Parsons, Talcott: *op. cit.*, pp. 29–30.
7. Nottingham, E. K.: *Methodism and the Frontier*, New York, Columbia University Press, 1941, p. 81.
8. Niebuhr, H. Richard: *Social Sources of Denominationalism*, New York, Henry Holt & Co., Inc., 1929, pp. 19, 20.
9. Pope, Liston: *Millhands and Preachers*, New Haven, Yale University Press, 1942, pp. 117–140.
10. La Piana, George: *Foreign Groups in Rome during the First Centuries of the Empire*, Cambridge, Harvard University Press, 1927, p. 340.
11. Smith, Luke M.: "Clergy: Authority Structure, Ideology, Migration," *American Sociological Review* 18:242–248 (June 1953).
12. Reported in Yinger, John M.: *op. cit.*, pp. 155–8.
13. Swift, Arthur: *New Frontiers of Religion*, New York, The Macmillan Company, 1938, pp. 113–4.

chapter seven

Religion in American Society

Chapter Six on religious organization and also the preceding discussion cites various illustrations drawn from the American scene. But all along we have considered the functions, organization, and changes of religious systems in a larger social and historical framework. Sociological generalization requires this procedure—requires, that is to say, study of various societies and cultures and diverse religions. A developed sociology of religion, it should be stressed, would demand far greater use of comparative materials than a work of this size permits. However, we have been able to suggest at least some answers in sociological—not religious—terms to such questions as the following: What are religion's most important functions in society? To what extent are they modified by social change? How and why does religion play a part in situations of stress? How does religion provide moral interpretations of political, economic, and class systems? What problems inhere in religious organization itself? How far and under what conditions have religious groups exerted influence upon society?

These questions, if directed to contemporary America, to some extent could guide a sociological investigation of religion in this country. But such a study would involve additional questions. For as we move from the general to the particular—say from a view of religion as such to religion in a particular time and place—our queries necessarily become more concrete and specific. The more general and abstract formulations will greatly enhance our understanding of the particular case if they are grounded in sound research; but the specific case always has its own peculiarities and, in some measure, its own explanation. This is true, of course, of religion in the United States.

In this concluding chapter we make no attempt to develop this theme fully. Our goal is limited and twofold. First, and this is the more concrete aspect, we shall consider briefly the relationship between Protestant Christianity and basic American values, interconnections between religion and the class system, and between religious organization and political democracy. We shall be concerned with functional contributions of religion to the stability of American culture and society and also with certain aspects of the dysfunctional role organized religion sometimes plays. These matters must of course be viewed in their specific social context. Secondly, however, we shall suggest interpretations here and there that stem from theoretical generalizations, for example, those of Max Weber, based upon studies of non-American situations.

We caution the reader that the following pages are an exceedingly limited treatment of religion in the United States. If interested in pursuing this subject, he will find available extensive historical and sociological materials, some of which are described briefly in the Selected Readings at the end of this study.

Protestant Christianity and the American Value System

Modern American values may seem to have little connection with religion. Yet many of those most familiar and important to us are more or less secularized versions of values of religious origin. American religious tradition was set in the country's formative years by the early Protestant settlers; therefore we must examine certain values emphasized by Protestant Christianity itself. We must also bear in mind that Protestantism, in common with all Christianity, contains much that is derived from the older tradition of Judaism and from the thought of ancient Greece.

Activism, universalism and *individualism*—three rather formidable abstractions—perhaps best summarize the secularized religious values that pervade American life.

Christianity, in common with Judaism, and in sharp contrast to Hinduism and Buddhism, ascribes a positive value to the natural material world. Though the Christian has a supreme other-worldly goal, nevertheless this world, including its material aspects, is positively valued as the scene of his active endeavors. This attitude toward the material world is especially strong in Protestant Christianity. The implication is not that the world as it is unrelievedly good—far from it—but that it is the God-given duty of man to master, control, and improve it for the glory of God and for his own benefit.

A second dominant characteristic of Christianity is that it views its truths as universal values. Thus Christians regard their truths as being equally true for all people, in all places, at all times. The ancient Greeks, moreover, had bequeathed to the Christian world the conception that the physical universe constitutes a challenge to the exploring intellect of man. It was but a further step to extend this universalistic attribute of Christian religious truths to truths about the natural world.

The concept of universal natural law is basic to modern science. It was probably no accident that the use of scientific means for the solution of human problems was initially most readily adopted in those countries influenced by Christianity with its universalistic conception of truth.[1] In spite of much modern talk about the conflict between religion and science it was Newton, a deeply religious man, who furnished science with a religious vindication by claiming that the supreme task of the scientist is "to know God through His Works."

When the notion of universal law is combined with the activist approach to the material world so characteristic of Calvinistic Protestantism, there results a powerful impetus to science and technology. Since early America was settled mainly by members of Calvinistic and independent Protestant sects who faced a natural environment that made heavy demands on their ingenuity, it is not surprising that achievements in science and technology became dominant values in American life. Science as well as religion has its missionaries; in our American tradition the Christian missionary has often set the pattern and paved the way for his scientific successor. With the Point Four and Technical Assistance Programs, the Fulbright, Rockefeller, and Ford Programs, the United States has a heavy interest in the spread of technological gospel in the world today—and is aided by the fact that technology speaks a universal language.

A third trait of Christianity, one given particular emphasis by Protestantism, is its stress on the individual. Individualism stems in part from the Christian idea of the individual soul, which gives a sacred value to each human being. Though Christianity has at times valued the ethereal soul at the expense of the earthly body, the belief that the body is the temple of the soul enables the value imputed to the soul to be extended to the totality of the individual. This concept of the supreme worth of the individual human being became a cornerstone of American democratic thought. Moreover, Protestant Christianity in particular emphasized the responsibility of each individual to take at least some independent initiative in regard to the salvation of his own soul.

Generally, the values of activism, universalism, and individualism have exercised a positive function in American society, helping to shape a tradition which has given unity, coherence, and stability to a society composed of diverse peoples. In spite of our many differences, these shared values increase our awareness of how we are expected to act towards one another as fellow Americans. This fact has been, and still is, of major importance for the maintenance of our society.

But to state that these values have a positive function in American society is by no means to claim perfection for them. Different sets of values may perform positive functions for different kinds of societies. Moreover, any cultural values are likely to have some negative, dysfunctional consequences in the society in which they prevail. For example, an unmitigated policy of active individualism in regard to the material world can lead to exploitation and waste of both our natural and human resources.

Religion and the American Class System

The ranking scale of any society is always closely related to those values which the society in question esteems most highly. American society is no exception. The high premium placed on successful individual achievement is fully in keeping with the values we have just discussed. In the semiopen class society that developed in the United States during the process of opening up a new continent individual success, as manifested by wealth and occupation, largely took the place of the Old World emphasis on family and inherited land as the principal requirement for high social standing. Hence the self-made man became a person not only of economic consequence, but of social prestige.

But it was also necessary to justify the self-made man. Religion has played an important part in this justification and has thereby helped to moralize our entire class system. In the same manner that religion has aided the Hindus to interpret the rigidities of their caste system, religion has provided moral justification to Americans for certain aspects of the American competitive class system—particularly the high premium placed on success and the consequent penalization of failure. Without this interpretation the successful might feel guilty about their success and the unsuccessful discouraged and resentful about their failures. Furthermore, given positive attitudes to the material world, it is not enough to claim that all moral imbalances will be rectified in heaven: it is crucial to interpret success as morally right—and failure as implying moral lack—here and now.*

---

* It is true of course that American Protestants have believed that the good are to receive their reward in heaven and the wicked their punishment in hell. But this other-worldly

We have already seen that the religious beliefs of the early Protestant settlers were well adapted to this type of interpretation, for their religion taught
them that God bestowed his especial favor on those individuals who strove
most actively and diligently in their this-worldly activities.* Success, then,
could be considered as the justly deserved reward of a man's purposeful, self-
denying, God-guided activity. Thus the *successful* man could think of himself, and be thought of by others, as the *righteous* man. These beliefs also
served to make moral sense of the plight of the so-called failures. Since religion
taught that the help of an all-powerful God is equally available to all, and
since all men if they will, can be diligent and thrifty, it is a man's own fault
if he fails. Even "failures" usually accepted the moral justice of this interpretation—an interpretation, be it noted, that did not deprive them of hope.
Furthermore, these religious doctrines were well suited to the circumstances
of a pioneer people, mostly of humble station, who had to rely on their own
resourcefulness to develop a new and potentially rich country.

Economic and social circumstances, however, have changed markedly since
those early days. Today impersonal economic and political forces, often beyond
the individual's control, are in part responsible for his failure or success. Yet
the older religious interpretations, more suited to earlier conditions, still persist in some measure. Illustrative of this persistence is the fact that during
the mass unemployment of the thirties the majority of one group of both
employed and unemployed when interviewed explained their respective economic situations almost entirely in individual moral terms. Most of those
employed attributed their success to their own superior efforts, implying that
anyone could have done as much with comparable effort. It is significant that
the unemployed and those on relief generally accepted this valuation, regarding
their failure as somehow their own fault.[2]

Yet changed circumstances eventually modify religious interpretations of
economic and class systems. The depression and its aftermath contributed to
such reinterpretations in the United States. Earlier we noted two aspects of
the individualism of Christianity. One is the emphasis on individual striving
and initiative, the other is the supreme valuation of each individual human
being. Sometimes, as during the depression, it has seemed necessary to limit
the insecurities and hardships to which some individuals were exposed even
at the cost of curtailing the initiative of others. In striving to guarantee to each
individual a minimal freedom from want the proponents of social security
legislation can also look to religious values for justification. Which of these
two interpretations of individualism is likely to be stressed at any given time
depends largely on the current state of the economy. The latter interpretation,

balancing of the moral books has been most stressed by those individuals and classes who
are least privileged and presumably most in need of compensation for their lack of success,
and therefore of status, in this world.

* According to Max Weber the Calvinist ethic was especially important in ascribing this
meaning to worldly success. However, some American historians, who agree in part with
Weber, contend that the independent Congregational, rather than the Calvinist, sects were
the main exponents of this ethic. Still other historians opine that the conditions of American
pioneer life, combined with the lowly class origin of most of the settlers, gave rise to the
ethic, rather than vice versa. None of these controversies need concern us here. We are
not interested, in this context, in priority of cause. It is sufficient for our purposes that
religion played a part. And there is no doubt that the religious ethic of the Protestant
settlers was consistent with, even congenial to, the actual conditions that they encountered.

justifying security measures, is perhaps less characteristically American, but nevertheless it is partly grounded in the Christian religion.*

Religious doctrines have thus served to justify the economic and class system—a fact that has contributed to the equilibrium of the system itself. Though the imputation of righteousness to the successful man has sometimes exercised a negative function—notably in condoning hypocrisy—yet it has also fulfilled a positive one in putting pressure on the successful man to act as if he were righteous. The fact that our Carnegies, Rockefellers, and Fords have not felt free, as have many successful capitalists in other countries, to dissipate their material gains in riotous living and what may be called "unproductive expenditure" has helped to stabilize and develop our economy. The investment of a substantial part of their gains in schemes for human betterment has also helped to soften some of the rigors of our competitive system and to spread its benefits. Even attributing failure to lack of moral stamina, as evidenced by the absence of hard work, enterprise, and thrift, is not a counsel of despair since such failure need not be permanent. This explanation encourages today's lower class folk to think of themselves as tomorrow's middle class, again contributing to the continuing stability of the class system.

Religious Organization and Democracy

The type of religious organization that has grown up in the United States is, on the whole, compatible with our political and industrial democracy. This compatibility is due in part to two related features of the American religious scene, both of which date from the early years of the Republic. The first is the separation of church and state: there is no powerfully established church or ecclesia. The second is the coexistence of a plurality of different denominations and sects, no single one of which is strong enough to exercise a predominant influence on the society as a whole. The variety of religious affiliations of the early settlers made expedient the toleration of people of all religious faiths, including Catholics and Jews, at an earlier date than in most European countries. In addition, the influence of French Revolutionary thought upon the founders of the American Republic helped to bring the separate secular state into existence sooner in America than in any other part of the Christian world.

This situation has had profound effects, both positive and permissive, upon the development of liberal democracy. On the positive side, has been the assertion on religious grounds by most Protestant groups of an active faith in democracy itself, especially those aspects of democracy which are expressed in the First Amendment. The liberal Protestant churches in particular, with their vigorous tradition of individual independence in religion initiated in colonial times by Roger Williams and developed further by Emerson and Thoreau, have endorsed this valuation. The freedom of the individual to choose and express his own religious and political beliefs without coercion has been a prime value for those churches. Generally they have regarded the opportunity afforded by America for people of wide religious differences to live together peacefully under the protection of a religiously neutral state as one of

---

* This second interpretation is more common in those branches of Christianity that have remained ecclesia. For example, the philosophy of the Anglican Church, with its emphasis on the welfare of an entire territorial community, is less hostile to socialism than is the American brand of Protestant Christianity.

the nation's greatest glories. These beliefs have also helped to make our country a haven for the religiously and politically oppressed. Churches which today continue actively to hold these beliefs are sensitive about any infringement of civil as well as religious liberties. Their members join organizations to protect the rights of minorities, whether racial, ethnic, or economic, and are easily alarmed if in their view any one church attempts to gain special privileges from the state.

On the permissive side, the lack of a single, united, and socially influential religious organization has facilitated the development of the United States as an "open society," that is, one free to pioneer in techniques and in ideas.[3] We have observed that religion can be very conservative. The same circumstances which precluded the development of an ecclesia also permitted wide experimentation in a number of fields exceedingly important to the character of the developing society. In all likelihood the United States could not have pushed on so fast and so far in industrial development, the application of science, the extension of free education to all ages and classes, and in the elaboration of political democracy, if the cultural tone had been set by a single dominant church. Talcott Parsons has noted the contrasting case of Quebec, where for the past three hundred years the Catholic Church has been the dominant ecclesia, and where until quite recently a society has persisted strikingly similar to that of rural France in the seventeenth century.

Furthermore, the absence of a dominant church has also helped to prevent American people from dividing into religious and antireligious camps.[4] Such a cleavage would have had important consequences for the political stability of American society. In this respect our political history of the last two centuries contrasts significantly with that of certain European countries, for example France and Russia. In the latter cases the social, economic, and intellectual changes that followed the industrial revolution occurred in societies possessing established churches, that is, ecclesiae. During the period of political upheavals ushered in by the French Revolution the once-dominant ecclesiae attempted to retain their influence by making common cause with the conservative vested interests and the landed classes. Hence the intellectuals and many members of the urban industrial classes became bitterly antireligious and anticlerical. In France the alignment of the antimonarchical with antireligious and anti-Catholic forces, so important during the revolutionary period, continues to set the tone of modern French radicalism. In Russia the alliance between the reactionary Czarist regime and the Orthodox Church (of which the Czar himself was the titular head) enabled Communism to thrive as a violently antireligious force and thus helped to precipitate the greatest revolution of our day. No comparable polarization of the population along religious and antireligious lines took place in the United States.

In contrast to many countries in continental Europe, outright hostility to religion in the United States is rare, though our society is highly secularized. Max Weber, who was familiar with the established Protestant Church in Germany, was surprised when he came to America in 1904 to find about 90 per cent of the population to be members of religious organizations, to which they contributed generously in spite of the fact that church membership was voluntary.[5] Even today, when the proportion of members to nonmembers is nearer 50 than 90 per cent, marginality, or indifference in regard to religious group membership, is more typical of Americans than hostility to organized religion. The fact that in the 1952 presidential election the candidates of both major parties were professed church members and presumably felt that endorsement of religion in general was expected of them by the majority of all voters, suggests that American society is far from being divided along religious and antireligious lines.

Difficulties and Tensions

Though voluntarism and denominational pluralism in religion have been congenial to the development of a democratic and industrial society, from the standpoint of religion there is a debit side to the account. American churches have been exposed to powerful secularizing influences. The United States stands in sharp contrast with England, for example, where a modified form of ecclesia has been able to utilize at least some of the government's influence in the fields of education, recreation, morals, and philanthropy. A plural system of religious organization coupled with rigid separation of church and state weaken religion's hold on the other institutions of the society.

In the United States the public school system, the most far-reaching educational agency, is directly dependent on the secular state; and, largely because of religious divisions, the teaching of religion in schools is prohibited. Similarly the control of recreation has passed in large part to commercial agencies. And the elaboration of the economic system has created such huge problems for social service and philanthropic organizations that much, though not all, of their ministration has also passed into governmental hands. In the face of this situation the churches have generally reacted rather than acted. They frequently struggle to hold their members by borrowing secular techniques. They try to compete with commercialized recreation by sponsoring their own, and to this end use motion pictures, radio, television, and the like. They also compete with mass communication specialists by presenting forums and book-review sessions, and by preaching popular sermons dealing with practical life and avoiding scientifically dubious dogmas. This growing use of secular methods has been dubbed the "basketballization" of the churches.[6] In spite of the use of such popular (and expensive) techniques, some churches have barely survived. To be sure, America's churches continue to bring religious and other benefits to thousands of individuals, an achievement which should not be underestimated. Nevertheless it must be admitted that the churches have mitigated rather than substantially modified criticized features of the economic and class system or checked the powerful trend of national states towards war. With the exigent demands of making a living, improving social status, paying taxes, and performing military service, most Americans are not overly preoccupied with religious matters.

The fact that religious organization reflects rather than sets the tone of American society is illustrated by the parallelism between social class divisions and denominational lines. In most American communities the churches have a rough rank order of social prestige. In New England the Unitarian and Episcopal churches are those of the "best people," followed by the Congregationalists and the Methodists, the Baptists, and other groups. In the South the Presbyterians take the place of the Unitarians, and in the Middle West the Methodists rank considerably higher. In New Orleans the Catholic descendants of the early French and Spanish settlers are among that city's leading families. One result of this social ranking of churches is the tendency of people who rise in the social scale to change their religious affiliation in the process.

Social ranking of religious denominations, to be sure, is consistent with the American open class system. Furthermore, since by their very nature Protestant congregations are rather loosely organized voluntary groups, they function best if their members feel at home with one another. This feeling of social ease is important in producing spontaneous consensus, which occurs much more readily when the members are of similar class and educational background. But a system of rank order of social prestige not only distresses sincere religionists[7] but, once established as a part of the community life, cannot be easily modified. Religious organizations whose participants experience their togetherness sacramentally more than socially, most notably the Catholic Church, have been the most effective in bringing together members of diverse social classes. The less inclusive character of Protestant churches also extends to racial and ethnic groups.

Immigrants to the United States, in accordance with constitutionally guaranteed principles of toleration for all religious groups, have brought with them their own traditional churches. Newcomers have made wide use of this freedom which has, indeed, provided an important means for preserving the cultures of their homelands. The migrations of the latter decades of the nineteenth century and of the early twentieth century brought large numbers of people from the peasant agricultural societies of southern and eastern Europe into our teeming cities, including many of the Roman Catholic, Greek Orthodox, and Jewish faiths. Organizationally, some of these churches differed markedly from American Protestantism, a situation which at times has given rise to both political and religious tensions.

The growth in power and influence of the Roman Catholic Church especially has stimulated problems associated with the fact that the Catholic Church is an ecclesia. An ecclesia, as we have seen, functions most harmoniously in societies of type two, whereas modern American urban society more nearly approximates type three. Traditionally the ecclesia is a universal church, comprising all the members of a given society and therefore accustomed to rely on the civil government for the endorsement of its authority. Though the central body of the Catholic Church in modern times has in practice modified this position, it has not abandoned it in principle. We know too that when Catholicism is dominant in a society, as in Spain, it tends to revert to the ecclesia pattern, abandon toleration of other religious groups, and assert its authority over the entire population.

Hence the rapid growth of the Catholic Church has occasioned some fear (whether the fear is well grounded is not the issue here) that with its increased power the Church will attempt to revive its ecclesia tradition in the United States. This fear is not unmixed with envy on the part of the Protestants, for in fields in which Protestantism is divided and weak the Catholic Church, with its unity of command, has superior effectiveness and has been able to retain a firmer hold on its adherents than have the more loosely organized Protestant churches. Furthermore, political differences have combined with religious ones to accentuate the tensions. Because of the heavy concentration of Catholics in the large cities of the East, the feeling of tension has been greatest there, and religious issues have frequently been acute in municipal politics. Since established local elites for the most part have been Protestant and since until recently the Catholics have been preponderant in the lower status groups, class tensions have been added to religious tensions. Moreover— and this is important in view of the leadership of the Irish in the Catholic Church in America—some of the traditional (and well-deserved) Old World hostility of the Irish towards the English may have colored American Catholic attitudes toward "Anglo-Saxon" Protestants.

Tensions may also be observed in connection with the stand taken by the Catholic Church on morals. According to Catholic religious organization and belief the hierarchy is empowered to regulate the morals of church members. In the United States, however, such regulation cannot always be effective without impinging on the freedom of choice of non-Catholics as well. On occasion some part of the moral code of the Church is enforced with the aid of state legislation, involving Catholics and non-Catholics alike. That Catholic voters should endeavor to introduce or to maintain legislation embodying the Church's stand on such matters as divorce and birth control is, of course, their constitutional right—a right they share with other groups. This right is not an issue here. But no sociologist can doubt that legislation maintaining the Catholic stand on divorce and birth control sets up in certain states legal standards powerfully at odds with dominant trends in the development of the American family structure, especially in large cities. The fact that these laws are at times circumvented by Catholics as well as non-Catholics further emphasizes this disparity.

In view of the existence of these strains, we would expect some degree of strong feeling and prejudice on the part of Catholics towards non-Catholics and vice versa. When such questions as state aid to parochial schools or legislation affecting the distribution of birth-control literature are under consideration, tempers get out of hand on both sides. Here sociology can play no useful role if it minimizes or obscures social realities. Its function rather is to bring out the cultural and structural determinants of prejudice and strain so that they may be understood as realistically as possible.

Difficulties between Jews and non-Jews far less than those between Catholics and non-Catholics are based on differences in religious organization. Anti-Semitism in the United States stems mainly from economic and cultural tensions—which have been the subject of extensive sociological analysis—and is not properly speaking a religious problem. Because of the ethnic character of Judaism, however, anti-Semitism in America is sometimes attributed to religious causes.

In point of fact, traditional patterns of Jewish religious organization accommodate themselves rather easily to the American scene, especially to denominational pluralism and the secular state. Basic to this adjustment is the fact that Judaism has no surviving tradition of an ecclesia, no central hierarchy, and no proselytizing tendencies. Its vital organizational unit is the synagogue or temple—a local congregation democratically governed. The authority of the rabbi receives considerably less institutional support than that of the average Protestant minister over his congregation. For the rabbi's function is not essential to the conduct of the synagogue, which for prayer, worship, and study requires only the existence of a *minyan*, namely a quorum of ten adult males who have been admitted to Bar Mitzvah. Moreover, since the Dispersion the Jewish people have constituted minority groups in almost every country of the world, and they have, putting it mildly, come to expect no preferential support from governments, particularly Christian ones. Therefore, the constitutional assurance of the benevolent neutrality of the secular state has great positive value for Jews, as well as for other groups.

In addition to organizational compatibility, from the doctrinal point of view there is little to distinguish Liberal Reform Judaism from liberal Protestantism. This suggests, once more, that tensions between Jews and non-Jews are only in small measure due to intrinsically religious differences.

In the absence of historical perspective, an objective estimate of the extent to which these cleavages and strains are functional or dysfunctional is impossible. On the other hand some of their consequences may be seen in the area of municipal politics and government. Decisions in this field are too often made, not on the objective merits of the persons or issues involved, but rather with a view to their possible effect on Catholic, Jewish, or Protestant interests, or with an eye to maintaining a balance between the different religious groups.

On the positive side, however, strains and disharmonies in the social structure may serve as stimuli for creative adaptations which may enable the structure to encompass a wider range of variations. There is evidence that to some extent this has already taken place in the United States and that the long-continued effort to achieve unity in diversity and order with freedom has been favorable to useful social and political experimentation. The tensions we have just described need not lead to disaster. If we can keep our social system sufficiently flexible and dynamic, we retain the possibility of absorbing these strains. Thus we may hope to preserve the most cherished values of our society.

Footnotes to Chapter Seven

1. Cf. Merton, Robert K.: Science, Technology and Society in Seventeenth Century England (Osiris Studies in the History and Philosophy of Science), Bruges, Belgium, St. Catherine Press, Ltd., 1938.
2. Calkins, Clinch: Some Folks Won't Work, New York, Harcourt, Brace & Co., 1930, especially pp. 7–22.
3. Cf. Parsons, Talcott: Religious Perspectives in College Teaching, New Haven, Edward W. Hazen Foundation, 1951, p. 35.
4. Ibid., p. 36.
5. Weber, Max: From Max Weber: Essays in Sociology. Edited and translated by H. H. Gerth and C. Wright Mills. New York, Oxford University Press, 1946, p. 302.
6. Page, Charles H.: "Bureaucracy and the Liberal Church," The Review of Religion, March 1952, pp. 147–8.
7. Cf. Niebuhr, H. Richard: Social Sources of Denominationalism, New York, Henry Holt & Co., Inc., 1929, pp. 6–10.

Selected Readings

General Works

CHINOY, ELY: *Sociological Perspective, Basic Concepts and Their Application* (Studies in Sociology) New York, Random House, Inc., 1954.
A useful and clear discussion of such concepts as culture, social structure, function, and social change.

MERTON, R. K.: *Social Theory and Social Structure*, Glencoe, Ill., The Free Press, 1949.
Chapter 1 is a basic reading in functional analysis; Chapters 14 and 15 treat the historical interconnections between religion and modern science.

PARSONS, TALCOTT: *The Structure of Social Action*, New York, McGraw-Hill Book Company, 1937; and *Religious Perspectives of College Teaching in Sociology and Social Psychology*, New Haven, Edward W. Hazen Foundation, 1951.
The first volume contains a detailed analysis of the views of Max Weber and Émile Durkheim (among others); the second is an outstanding essay in the sociology of religion.

WILSON, LOGAN, and W. L. KOLB: *Sociological Analysis*, New York, Harcourt, Brace & Co., 1949.
The distinction between types of societies made in Chapter 11 are similar to those drawn in this study; Chapter 19 contains useful readings on religious organization.

Landmark Studies in the Sociology of Religion

DURKHEIM, ÉMILE: *The Elementary Forms of the Religious Life.* Translated by J. W. Swain. Glencoe, Ill., The Free Press, 1947.
Originally published in 1902, this volume, based in part on Spencer and Gillen's study of an Australian tribe, is the outstanding pioneer work on the social aspects of religious beliefs and practices.

MALINOWSKI, BRONISLAW: *Magic, Science and Religion*, Glencoe, Ill., The Free Press, 1948. (Reprinted as an Anchor Book, 1954.)
The first part of this volume is a brilliant essay on magic, science, and religion, drawing on illustrations from the Trobrianders, so thoroughly studied by Malinowski.

TAWNEY, R. H.: *Religion and the Rise of Capitalism*, New York, Harcourt, Brace & Co., 1936. (Reprinted as a Mentor Book, 1948.)
An elaboration as well as critique of Weber's work, listed below.

WEBER, MAX: *The Protestant Ethic and the Spirit of Capitalism*. Translated by T. Parsons. London, George Allen and Unwin, 1930; and *From Max Weber: Essays in Sociology*. Translated and edited by H. H. Gerth and C. Wright Mills. New York, Oxford University Press, 1946.

The first volume is a classic research and analysis of historical relations between Protestantism and modern capitalism; the second, in Parts 3 and 4, contains further material on Weber's well-known thesis.

Religion in Nonliterate Societies

GOODE, W. J.: *Religion among the Primitives*, Glencoe, Ill., The Free Press, 1951.

A detailed functional analysis of comparative materials drawn from cultural anthropology.

HOWELLS, WILLIAM: *The Heathens, Primitive Man and His Religions*, New York, Doubleday & Company, Inc., 1948.

An exceedingly readable book, exploring such topics as the nature of religion, mana, and taboo, and magic in its various forms.

KLUCKHOHN, CLYDE: *Navaho Witchcraft*, Cambridge, Mass., Peabody Museum of American Archaeology and Ethnology, 1944.

A field study by a team of social anthropologists and psychiatrists of the social and psychological functions of Navaho witchcraft.

Religion in Literate Societies

FRIESS, HORACE L., and HERBERT W. SCHNEIDER: *Religion in Various Cultures*, New York, Henry Holt & Co., Inc., 1932.

A useful account, from the standpoint of religion, of the development of Hinduism, Buddhism, Confucianism, Islam, and other religions of the world.

NOSS, JOHN: *Man's Religions*, New York, The Macmillan Company, 1950.

A good introduction to the study of comparative religion.

Religion and the American Scene

ABRAMS, RAY H. (Ed.): "Organized Religion in the United States," *The Annals* of the American Academy of Political and Social Science, March, 1948.

A highly useful collection, including articles on religion as a social institution, churches and the class system, the sects, and brief essays on Protestantism, Catholicism, and Judaism.

FAUSET, A. H.: *Black Gods of the Metropolis*, Philadelphia, University of Pennsylvania Press, 1944.

A revealing field study of five expressive cults and sects in Philadelphia, including Father Divine's Peace Mission.

FICHTER, J. H.: *Southern Parish*, Chicago, University of Chicago Press, 1951.

A detailed field study by a Jesuit parish priest of parochial organization in a city in the deep South.

NOTTINGHAM, E. K.: *Methodism and the Frontier: Indiana Proving Ground*, New York, Columbia University Press, 1941.

A sociohistorical account of the growth of Methodism from sect to denomination in early nineteenth century Indiana.

Pope, Liston: *Millhands and Preachers*, New Haven, Yale University Press, 1942.
A sociological study of the dynamics of the growth of new sects in mill villages in the South.

Sperry, W. L.: *Religion in America*, New York, The Macmillan Company, 1946.
An intelligent, lucid description of religion in the United States written for the purpose of explaining that subject to Englishmen by the Dean of Harvard's Theological School.

Yinger, J. M.: *Religion in the Struggle for Power*, Durham, N.C., Duke University Press, 1946.
An application of the theories of Weber and Troeltsch to an analysis of the effectiveness of religious organization in modern America.